The New York Times

Guide to
Business Communication

Mary Ellen Guffey

Jamie Murphy

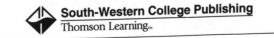

South-Western College Publishing
Thomson Learning™

Australia • Canada • Denmark • Japan • Mexico • New Zealand • Philippines
Puerto Rico • Singapore • South Africa • Spain • United Kingdom • United States

The New York Times Guide to Business Communication,
by Mary Ellen Guffey & Jamie Murphy

Publisher: Dave Shaut
Acquisitions Editor: Pamela M. Person
Marketing Manager: Rob Bloom
Production Editor: Elizabeth A. Shipp
Media and Technology Editor: Kevin von Gillern
Media Production Editor: Robin K. Browning
Manufacturing Coordinator: Sandee Milewski
Internal Design: Joe Devine
Cover Design: Joe Devine
Production House: Trejo Production
Printer: Webcom

For more information contact South-Western College Publishing, 5101 Madison Road,
Cincinnati, Ohio, 45227 or find us on the Internet at http://www.swcollege.com
For permission to use material from this text or product, contact us by
• **telephone: 1-800-730-2214**
• **fax: 1-800-730-2215**
• **web: http://www.thomsonrights.com**

Library of Congress Cataloging-in-Publication Data

Guffey, Mary Ellen
   The New York Times guide to business communication / Mary Ellen Guffey, Jamie
Murphy.
      p. cm.
      ISBN 0-324-04161-6 (alk. paper)
      1. Business writing. 2. English language—Business English. 3. Business
communication.   I. Murphy, Jamie, 1950–   II. Title.

HF5718.3 .G843 1999
808'.06665--dc21   99-052892

This book is printed on acid-free paper.

P R E F A C E

The New York Times Guide to Business Communication is designed for students, professors and business professionals—anyone interested in staying current in business today. A collection of the best business communication-related articles from the *New York Times*, this guide does more than inform: it also provides context for the effects of change on all aspects of business. Also included are articles from *CyberTimes*, the online-only technology section of the *New York Times on the Web*. Each article was selected for its relevance to today's business world.

In purchasing *The New York Times Guide to Business Communication*, you are not only purchasing the contents between the covers, but also unlimited access, via password, to related *New York Times* articles. Current articles will be linked from the South-Western College Publishing/*New York Times* Web site (http://nytimes.swcollege.com) on an ongoing basis as news breaks.

This guide can be used formally in the classroom or informally for life-long learning. All articles are accompanied by exploratory exercises and probing questions developed by experts in the field. Previews provide context for each chapter of articles and link them to key business communication principles. This guide is divided into seven sections organized to highlight the seven most critical factors in business communication today. This organization allows for easy integration into any business communication course.

Chapter 1: Communicating Effectively in Today's Business Environment. This opening chapter underscores the need for effective communication and brings you up to speed on today's fast-paced business communication environment. Topics include: communication foundations, listening, non-verbal communication, time management, multitasking, e-mail, distance learning, cultural diversity and presentation skills.

Chapter 2: Changing Technology and Business Communication. A lesson from history and a glance into the future help you understand technology's influence on business communication. Topics include: communication foundations, business communication technology, convergence, information and business communication standards.

Chapter 3: Legal and Ethical Issues Influencing Business Communication. As this chapter explains, today's technologies add digital dilemmas to the legal and ethical issues facing business communications. Topics include: privacy, employee monitoring, e-mail, personal information, workplace environment, ethics and legal concerns.

Chapter 4: Business Communication Tools—Old and New. There are numerous business communication tools available today, many of which are new within the last decade; many have been around forever. Topics include: business communication technology, e-mail, chat, customer communication, appropriate communication, penmanship and the writing process.

Chapter 5: Internet Business Communication Skills. Communicating today requires a basic understanding of the proper use, as well as misuse, of the Internet's two most popular business communication tools, e-mail and the World Wide Web. Topics include: e-mail, netiquette, the World Wide Web, the writing process, information sources, information searching, spam, letters, memos, report planning and research.

Chapter 6: Communication to Persuade. To be effective in business today you must be able to influence others to accomplish your objectives. In this chapter, you will see an example of how to persuade your boss that you should telecommute. Topics include: persuasion, telecommuting, the writing process, letters and memos.

Chapter 7: Career Communication. What is the best way to communicate to make your career search successful? Technology opens up new ways to search for employment. Learn the appropriateness of using new technologies in your career communications. Topics include: reports, proposals, the writing process, presentation skills, business communication technology and employment communication.

PEDAGOGICAL FEATURES

Critical Thinking Questions challenge you to form your own opinion about current topics. These questions can be used to stimulate classroom discussion or as the basis for formal assignments.

Short Application Assignments work well as hands-on exercises for both classroom discussion and formal assignments. Most assignments should take no more than a few hours to complete. Typical assignments include developing presentations and writing one-page memos, reports, executive summaries and articles for company newsletters.

Building Research Skills exercises allow you to expand upon what you have learned from the *New York Times'* articles and explore the unlimited resources available to enhance your understanding of current events. Typical assignments include presentations, writing essays and building Web pages.

Additional Online Pedagogy

Sample Exercises provide examples for you to follow in completing assignments.

Additional Readings link to more than 100 additional stories, categorized by chapter, for further research.

Writers on Writing is a series in which writers explore literary themes. Contributors include John Updike, E. L. Doctorow, Jane Smiley, Sue Miller, Annie Proulx and Kurt Vonnegut, Jr.

Book Reviews contains about 80 computers and digital technology books reviewed by the *New York Times*, listed alphabetically by author and linked to the original review.

ACKNOWLEDGMENTS

My sincere appreciation goes to co-author, Mary Ellen Guffey, for her prompt feedback and guidance, as well as to Carol M. Lehman and Debbie D. DuFrene for their help selecting stories and crafting the pedagogy. Special recognition for patience and understanding goes to editors I've had the opportunity to work with: Dr. Brian L. Massey, Nanyang Technological University, Singapore; Rob Fixmer and John Haskins, the *New York Times*; Jason Fry, the *Wall Street Journal*, Glenn Withiam, the *Cornell Hotel and Restaurant Administration Quarterly*; and Margaret Leonard, the *Florida State Times*.

This pioneering publishing project would not have been possible without the progressive thinking of the *New York Times* (Mike Levitas, Hilda Cosmo, Melanie Rosen, Christine M. Thomson, John Haskins and Jim Mones) and South-Western College Publishing (Pamela Person, Dave Shaut, Libby Shipp and Kevin von Gillern).

On a personal note, thanks to my lovely wife, Debbie, for her encouragement; my rambunctious children, Casey and Jamie, for letting me work in peace; my parents, Joan and Brannen, for their support; and my cyber-colleagues, Drs. Charles F. Hofacker, C. Edward Wotring and Edward J. Forrest, for their inspiration.

C O N T E N T S

Communicating Effectively in Today's Business Environment

PREVIEW

Paradoxically, effective communication in today's technological environment builds from an old-fashioned, technology-free foundation. Technology complements, but can never replace requisite soft skills, such as initiative, appearance, non-verbal communication, interpersonal communication, working well under pressure and time management. At the same time, technology creates a dynamic new business communication environment. Multi-modal, multi-media communication is the rule, rather than the exception. The Internet shrinks traditional communication barriers, time and distance. An emerging trend in this new environment is increased cultural diversity.

"Soft skills," as Sabra Chartrand explains in "A World Where Language and 'Soft Skills' Are Key," continue to be a key element of effective business communication. Amy Harmon illustrates two of these skills, time management and working under pressure in "Talk, Type, Read E-Mail: The Trials of Multitasking."

Multitasking fits in well with the trend today, diverse groups of employees working at "virtual" organizations. In "When a Company Splits Its Identity," Debra Nussbaum investigates the inevitable culture clashes as organizations cope with growth in a diverse business environment.

Adam Gwosdof, above, likes to use pay phones in pairs, retrieving voice-mail messages on one and returning calls on the other.

Source: Suzanne DeChillo/The New York Times

A World Where Language and 'Soft Skills' Are Key

By Sabra Chartrand

Language: A systematic way of arranging symbols, usually to express meaning. It may be a natural language like Chinese, English or Swahili that humans use to communicate with one another, or a programming language in which programs are written for a computer.

— Michael A. Arbib
Professor of computer science,
University of Southern California

In recent years it seems that language as it relates to software programming has come to be worth more in the job market than a mastery of English or Chinese. But natural language isn't just the gift of the gab. It's also a talent necessary for communication, which is distinct from mere conversation. Communication can be verbal or written. In the working world, the ability to communicate well is known as a soft skill. Soft skills have always been critical to professions like journalism, advertising or medicine. Now they're proving to be just as important to high-tech industries and businesses.

Effective communication isn't the only soft skill employers crave. Interpersonal skills, like the ability to create and maintain a rapport with others, are high on the list, too. Time management, initiative, working well under pressure, and image or appearance—especially as it bears on non-verbal communication—are also essential.

Technology has meant the blurring of traditional lines between workers and departments at many companies, particularly small, information technology start-ups. Businesses are less departmentalized. E-mail, for example, now allows all kinds of workers and managers to communicate directly with one another. Technical support staff who once worked in obscurity may now interact daily with sales and marketing staff, and with customers and clients.

Obviously, employers want programmers or developers who are at the top of their technical game. But increasingly, they also want employees who can articulate their goals clearly, write evocatively, work well with others and build relationships, take initiative, and represent a company's image of itself.

Soft skills—or, as they might have been called in another era, people skills.

Yet what does "effective communication" mean? First, understand that it can be verbal, non-verbal or written. Communication can include telephone links, telecommunication exchanges, E-mail, the Internet or writing reports. Thus, communication and conversation are not the same animal. But at the same time, language experts say conversation is often more than 90 percent non-verbal. Words alone make up only a tiny portion of the messages people send one another.

In his *Dictionary of Cybernetics*, Klaus Krippendorff, of the Annenberg School of Communications at the University of Pennsylvania, writes that non-verbal communication is "processes of communication without the use of language proper."

"Body movements, gesture, smells but also such extra-linguistic features of speech as intonation, speed, pause," Krippendorff said. "Non-verbal communication is expressive and manifest as opposed to being about something outside the communicator. Non-verbal communication tends to provide the context of verbal communication and has the power to disambiguate (but also to invalidate) the content of linguistic expressions."

So the way we talk—our speech patterns, our expressions, our eye movements—are critical to providing the context and clarity that words alone cannot. But how does the average worker learn to do this well?

Unfortunately, most of the large, popular career and job sites on the World Wide Web are devoted to finding, applying for and winning a new job. Most do not tell workers who already have a job how to improve their soft skills.

Smaller, and more obscure, subject-specific sites exist, but you have to hunt for them. Leading Edge Communications, for example, has a site devoted to promoting publications and seminars on effective business communication. But it also offers an intriguing page of written exercises designed to teach people to communicate better. The Writing Center also offers books and seminars on writing better at work, and the Summer Institute for Languages offers a tutorial on what constitutes written communication.

What else can a worker do? First, seek out a mentor among project leaders, managers or other more senior, more experienced colleagues. Second, many businesses offer communications, assertiveness and team-building training courses. In addition, some career and recruiting experts advise clients to take public speaking classes, sign up for writing courses through university extension programs, and even try out for community theater. Also, though many people who already have jobs think an employment agency or career counselor has nothing to offer them, such consultants often advise on communication, interpersonal and image strategies.

Image? Appearance can be an important part of soft skills. Remember that most communication is non-verbal. That can certainly be true during a job interview. An interviewer may become your new boss or colleague, and, as everyone knows, comes to an opinion about you based in part on appearance. Interviewers want to hire applicants with the best shot of fitting into the company's culture—and most workplaces have a distinct culture. Appearance, from the way a candidate dresses to his body language, can tell an interviewer a lot about an applicant's background, education, personality and outlook.

In fact, soft skills may be a deciding factor at a job interview, which is often the venue for an employer to test a candidate's communication or interpersonal skills. Can this candidate clearly and eloquently express his goals, or his ideas of how he will contribute to the company if hired? When asked how he would solve a technical problem, is his answer well-expressed and easy to understand? How much input did he have on projects at previous jobs and what kind of leadership roles did he take—meaning, did he take initiative, work well with a team, and communicate frequently during the old assignment? Does he establish a rapport with the interviewer and others he meets during the hiring process? Does he seem able to build relationships? Can he provide some writing samples?

Recruiters and employment specialists say that in the last few years, a job applicant's performance in these areas has weighed more heavily in the decision of who to hire. In a survey last year, RHI Consulting, a high-tech recruiting firm, asked information technology managers what they looked for in employees. RHI says 85 percent responded that they want "well-developed soft skills," and 68 percent believe those soft skills are more important now than five years ago.

CyberTimes, The New York Times on the Web, April 6, 1997
http://www.nytimes.com/library/jobmarket/040697sabra.html

CRITICAL THINKING QUESTIONS

1. When is communication different from conversation?
2. What does "effective communication" mean?
3. What could be considered non-verbal communication?
4. What functions could non-verbal communication serve?
5. How can you improve your soft skills?

SHORT APPLICATION ASSIGNMENTS

1. In teams of three to five, or as a class, discuss your responses to the preceding critical thinking questions.
2. Prepare a one-page memo report (200–250 words) to your instructor in which you respond to the critical thinking questions and offer a final summary of the article. You will find a model one-page report on the Web site (nytimes.swcollege.com).
3. Write an executive summary (200–250 words). As an administrative assistant to a busy executive, you are expected to summarize selected articles and present important points. You will find a model executive summary on the Web site.
4. Summarize this article (100–125 words) for your company's newsletter. You will find a model newsletter article on the Web site.
5. Review one or more of the "soft-skill" Web sites mentioned in the story. What did you find useful? Your instructor may ask you to share your results in a five-minute presentation or one-page memo.

BUILDING RESEARCH SKILLS

1. Using at least three other references (books, journal articles, newspaper stories, magazine stories or credible Web sites) write an 800- to 1,000-word essay addressing two of the preceding critical thinking questions.
2. Using at least three other references (books, journal articles, newspaper stories, magazine stories or credible Web sites) post an 800- to 1,000-word Web page addressing at least two of the preceding critical thinking questions.

Talk, Type, Read E-Mail:
The Trials of Multitasking

By Amy Harmon

It's hard for Michael Redd to say just when doing one thing at a time became so deeply dissatisfying. His ratings with customers have certainly soared since he started responding to their e-mail as soon as it chimes in, no matter if he is on the phone or eating lunch or poring over a spreadsheet on some other screen.

But his fondness for multitasking is not limited to the workplace. Redd, a 30-year-old manager at McDonald's corporate office in Oak Ridge, Ill., is happiest when his attention is most divided, like on a recent weekend afternoon when he watched a movie on television while talking to his sister and writing on his laptop. During commercial breaks, he flipped through his CD jukebox with a remote control, searching for a song whose name he had forgotten.

"I need to be able to do many things at once all the time," Redd said. "This may sound strange, but it makes me feel better."

Actually, it doesn't sound so strange. Multitasking—the word describes how a microprocessor keeps lots of computer programs running at the same time—has lately become a way of life for many Americans. Inundated with more information than ever before and—perhaps perversely—prone to equate productivity with pleasure, many people are quietly adapting the rhythms of their own behavior to match that of their machines.

As a result, the number of tasks to which people are simultaneously applying themselves is multiplying like some mutant breed of postmodern rabbit. The shift is driven by the seductive suggestion implicit in the latest high-tech tools that they can be used not only for the pedestrian purposes of communication and information retrieval but also to swindle time.

Some, like Redd, thrill to the challenge of prying more minutes out of a day. Others decry the increasing fragmentation of mind and soul that the technology seems to demand. But as the trill of cellular phones and beepers and signals for arriving e-mail have grown more persistent, they have also become harder to ignore.

"You can't be as focused," said Adam Gwosdof, 31. When Gwosdof uses pay phones, he finds a bank of them where he can monopolize two lines at once—one to listen to his messages and one to call the people who have left them. "You feel like you're always trying to conceal the amount of tasks you're juggling," he said. "It does create a real anxiety, and it's hard sometimes to even put your finger on what it is. It's knowing I can't ever be done or shut things out."

Gwosdof runs a database design business in Manhattan and often finds himself being paged by one client while meeting with another and using the Internet to check on a third. He prefers to work on five projects at once so he can plug gaps of time that might otherwise be wasted. He insists that he can scan Internet newsgroups "subconsciously" while he talks to friends on the phone.

But Gwosdof has recently been rethinking the way his life is structured. He attended a seminar on time management, although he arrived late and left early.

"We can't just jump back and forth hundreds of times without it taking a toll on the psyche," he said, returning a reporter's page by using, he said, just one pay phone.

Inherently elastic and often covert, the true extent of human multitasking is difficult to measure, but anecdotal evidence abounds. "You know what, I have to go out, but I can do this from my car," said Toby Crabel, 43, preparing to respond to a reporter's inquiry on the subject. "I'll call you back in three minutes."

Crabel credits technology with allowing him to run a hedge fund out of his house in the middle of some cornfields northwest of Milwaukee. He has programmed his network of computers so that when he is reading to his daughter Kira, 8, he can be prompted by a digitized female voice that it is time to buy Treasury bonds.

Microsoft says the average office user of Windows 95 has more than three programs running at a time. At home, more than 10 million American households now have a television and a personal computer in the same room.

"This is not new, but it is accelerating," said John Robinson, director of a project at the University of Maryland devoted to gauging Americans' use of time. "You can't expand time, so what you try to do is deepen time by doing more things in the same period."

Less clear is multitasking's effects on the people who do it and those around them.

Consider the argument that erupts at least once a day between David Kohn and his fiancée, Natasha Lesser, who confer by phone from their respective Manhattan offices on such issues as what to have for dinner.

"It's the clicking sound that sets me off," said Kohn, 31. "Then she starts pausing between words."

Ms. Lesser, 29, an editor at Fodor's Travel Publications, said she has tried to restrain herself since it bothers him so much, but the fact is she has a lot of work to do. "Some of the things I have to do don't require me to think, so I feel, why can't I talk and do them at the same time? Otherwise I'd be here till 10 at night."

Nor is it entirely clear whether Kohn, who sits in front of a bank of 16 televisions and a computer with a high-speed connection to the Internet for his job as a producer for the CBS Web site, is always as unwaveringly riveted to his conversations with Ms. Lesser as he makes out. The couple are still planning to get married in October. But both agree it is an ongoing problem. "We have discussed it," Kohn said. "At length."

To be sure, Americans are renowned for being obsessed with time, and multitasking was a time-honored human behavior well before Alt-Tab could zip you between, say, writing a newspaper article and reading up on a New York Police Department sex scandal in nary a microsecond. Women have long known about multitasking, as in the old song about bringing home the bacon, frying it up in a pan and never, ever letting you forget you're a man. Some men have demonstrated a capacity to walk and chew gum at the same time. Others have not.

What is different now, modern multitaskers observe, is how closely human conduct is tied to our technological tools, particularly to the PC. The tasks we find ourselves attending to, however briefly, are often determined by what pops up on our screen. On either a PC or Macintosh, windows of one sort or another beg for us to open them. And since our computer manages to keep them all humming at the same time, why shouldn't we?

For one thing, computers do not actually do more than one thing at once. The genesis of computer multitasking was in the early 1960's, when John McCarthy, who was then a computer scientist at the Massachusetts Institute of Technology, suggested that instead of one person at a time feeding data from punch cards into a mainframe, 50 people could use the mainframe simultaneously. Every time a different user entered a command, the machine would stop what it was doing, store it, perform the new task—for perhaps a millisecond—and so on.

"The radical idea was that you could work at your own desk because the machine could tolerate constant interruption," said McCarthy, now a professor emeritus at Stanford University. "Even in those days, the machine could handle 100 instructions in 2.4 milliseconds so it was just a question of doing the arithmetic."

When mainframes shrank into PC's in the early 1980's, multitasking was temporarily forsaken. Until fairly recently, the most widely used computer operating systems did not allow more than one program to run at a time. But today PC's work on the same principle as the time-sharing schemes for the mainframe, albeit with only one user issuing many commands.

So while your computer seems to be downloading e-mail, spell-checking and playing solitaire with you at the same time, it is in fact doing each of them serially. It is, however, doing them really, really fast. A relatively slow computer with a 100-megahertz processor can execute a million instructions between each pair of keystrokes by a very fast typist. And while a context switch—the computer term for saving one program in its current state while tending to another—requires a significant chunk of processing power, computers seem better able to weather the psychological toll of constant interruption.

"They switch faster than we do," said Earl Hunt, a professor of psychology and computer science at the University of Washington. "It's hard to get around the forebrain bottleneck." It seems that although people can do some highly practiced tasks simultaneously, like juggling and riding a unicycle, in general they can pay attention to only one thing at a time without overtaxing short-term memory.

"Our brains function the same way the Cro-Magnon brains did so technology isn't going to change that," Professor Hunt said. "You can do several tasks at once, but not all of them get done as well. That is why I feel that car phones are a bad idea."

Of course, not all jobs need to be done as well as others. One of the joys of multitasking, and perhaps one of its perils, is that it allows the blending of work and leisure in a way that was not possible before. Many multitaskers describe a sense of well-being that comes from the variety of tasks they are performing and the control they feel they exercise over which one comes first.

Ellen Ullman, author of *Close to the Machine,* about her life as a programmer, said she had tried to stop herself from sliding into the back-and-forth of multitasking on her computer at the expense of the softer-focus shifting of levels of attention more natural for humans.

"If you've ever watched someone who is a mother talk on the phone, feed the dog, bounce the baby, it's just astounding to see someone manage more or less well to do all those things," Ms. Ullman said. "But on a computer, multitasking is really binary. The task is either in the foreground or it's not. And now we are beginning to emulate the coarse-grain multitasking of computers that is a poor imitation of our own."

To the extent that multitasking depends on a certain prowess at filtering huge amounts of information without actually absorbing all of it, there is reason to believe that a generation that is growing up watching "Celebrity Death Match" on MTV while instant-messaging one another on America On-line may be better at it than their elders. Observing the awesome multitasking skills of the younger traders at Bankers Trust, Marc Prensky, a vice president there, has advocated a new management approach for them.

"If people are really good at processing information from lots of different sources and you don't give it to them, you stifle them," said Prensky, an avid multitasker himself. "I think it's a real sea change. We should understand it first and then use it to our advantage."

For Jai Mani, an 11-year-old in Manhattan, it's all a bit simpler. The urge to multitask is like "a craving for food."

When he gets home from rollerblading camp, he wants to do three things. "Instead of listening to music for 30 minutes, watching TV for 30 minutes and checking your e-mail for 30 minutes, you can do them all at the same time," said Jai, who has been known to watch television and keep an eye on his computer game in the high-gloss reflection of the piano while having a lesson. "It's just easier that way."

The New York Times, July 23, 1998
http://www.nytimes.com/library/tech/98/07/circuits/articles/23task.html

CRITICAL THINKING QUESTIONS

1. How does multitasking influence business communication?
2. Is multitasking a current phenomena or has it existed for ages?
3. Does multitasking make one more or less productive? Why, or why not?
4. Do certain traits—such as sex, race, age or access to technology—influence multi-tasking?

SHORT APPLICATION ASSIGNMENTS

1. In teams of three to five, or as a class, discuss your responses to the preceding critical thinking questions.
2. Prepare a one-page memo report (200–250 words) to your instructor in which you respond to the critical thinking questions and offer a final summary of the article. You will find a model one-page report on the Web site (nytimes.swcollege.com).
3 Write an executive summary (200–250 words). As an administrative assistant to a busy executive, you are expected to summarize selected articles and present important points. You will find a model executive summary on the Web site.
4. Summarize this article (100–125 words) for your company's newsletter. You will find a model newsletter article on the Web site.
5. Experiment with multitasking. What communication tasks can you perform simultaneously? How does multitasking influence your communication? Your instructor may ask you to share your results in a five-minute presentation or one-page memo.

BUILDING RESEARCH SKILLS

1. Using at least three other references (books, journal articles, newspaper stories, magazine stories or credible Web sites) write an 800- to 1,000-word essay addressing two of the preceding critical thinking questions.
2. Using at least three other references (books, journal articles, newspaper stories, magazine stories or credible Web sites) post an 800- to 1,000-word Web page addressing at least two of the preceding critical thinking questions.

When a Company Splits Its Identity

By Debra Nussbaum

This is the tale of two offices.

Together, they make up US Interactive, a digital marketing company that creates World Wide Web sites, intranets and other computer marketing communications for more than 300 companies. Half of the 100 employees work in the company's New York City office; the other half work in Malvern, Pa., a suburb of Philadelphia. Senior management is divided between the two.

Though just 106 miles apart, the staffs often seem to operate in separate universes. They work together on projects like Web sites for Martha Stewart and Royal Caribbean International. But their work hours, office spaces, commutes and job cultures are drastically different.

In New York, the office is the top floor of a renovated hotel at 49 West 27th St., off Sixth Avenue. It is open and airy, with hardwood floors, big windows and high ceilings. The conference room is on the roof level.

In Malvern, the staff works in a suburban office park, with more small offices and cubicles. Carpeting, in muted tones of green and mauve, abounds.

In New York, many employees come to work at 10 A.M. and are still there at 8 P.M. In Malvern, the work day starts at 7:30 or 8 A.M. and is often done by 6 P.M.

In New York, three-quarters of the employees are single, while in Malvern, the majority are married. In New York, only 19 percent of the employees have children; in Malvern, 38 percent do.

"Our daily lives are different from the time we wake up in the morning until we go to bed at night," said Michael Chaney, a managing partner in New York. "They drive to work. They're married. They have time pressures we don't have."

Culture clashes are most noticeable when big companies merge, but experts say some of the sharpest conflicts can be found at young companies experiencing rapid growth. Such firms must learn to manage operations of separate offices as they try to blend them into a unified whole.

As companies rely more on technology than human contact for interoffice communication and create branches with different hours and styles, such conflicts become common, said Barry Lawrence, spokesman for the Society for Human Resource Management, a professional trade group in Alexandria, Va.

US Interactive "is a microcosm of what's going on," he said. "I don't think any of us realized how important human contact was until we tried to strip it out."

Another company with growing pains was Ad One Classified Network, based in New York City. The company started in 1994 with four employees in one office; there are now 35 employees in four cities.

"The issue was how you put faces to the names," said Martha J. Glantz, a human resources consultant with Buck Consultants, in New York, who worked with Ad One. "They realized technology was good, but you were going to make it with good people."

The company built a Web site so employees could introduce themselves to one another electronically. To bring the staff together, it scheduled sales force meetings four times a year in different offices.

Brendan Burns, an Ad One founder, said investment in communications "is one of those things that, if you're not doing it, it leads to your demise."

The history of US Interactive's two offices goes back to the company's founding by Richard Masterson, a former marketing executive at Reynolds Metal, and Larry Smith, an account director at the New York ad agency Messner Vetere Berger McNamee Schmetterer Euro RSCG. The pair started the concern in 1991 out of their homes—Smith's in New York City, Masterson's in Medford, N.J.

From the outset, they sought clients in both markets. The New York office opened in late 1995; one in Philadelphia opened months later, then moved to Malvern to be closer to other high-technology firms. The business kept growing through acquisition—last year it bought Mixed Media Works of Blue Bell, Pa., with 20 employees and 100 clients and projects—and through the infusion of venture capital.

About a year ago, said Masterson, now the company's executive vice president for business development, he realized that the two offices were headed in different directions.

"There wasn't one specific incident that moved the needle," he said, though he recalled being surprised last year when he traveled to the New York office for a client meeting. Outside the conference room, the client was surrounded by people. At first, Masterson said, he thought it was the client's entourage. Then he realized that they worked for him, staffers whom he had not yet met.

"There was duplication of efforts that started to emerge," Masterson said. "There were the beginnings of an 'us versus them.' "

Other signs: In meetings, one office would discuss topics of which the other was unaware. "A shorthand was developing between employees geographically," he said.

Smith, who is based in New York and is the company's president, noticed a growing chill in dealings with the Malvern office. "We'd be talking about the same topic and having two different conversations," he said. "People had a lack of appreciation for each other."

Then came a telephone conference in which a New York manager yelled at a Malvern account manager, upsetting the Malvern office. "He didn't know how much damage had been caused by this call," Masterson said.

There was also a perception in Malvern's creative department that New York didn't trust it enough to share good work.

Debra Nussbaum

"If you work anywhere else besides New York, you're not creative," was how Dalia Pintel, an art director in Malvern, described the attitude. She said a designer in the New York office once asked her, "How can you create out here?"

Masterson said he was most concerned about the discussions that were not occurring: "It's like a bad marriage—it's not really the fighting that kills you; it's the silence."

Last spring, Masterson and Smith decided to push for change. They solicited staff suggestions for bridging the growing chasm.

Part of the solution was middle ground—New Jersey. Departments like the two creative staffs held lunch meetings about halfway between the offices, in the Princeton area. The company picnic was set for a halfway point on a workday, so more people could attend.

The company bought tickets to a Yankees-Phillies interleague baseball game last year in Philadelphia and invited both staffs to attend. (The day after the game, won by the Phillies, there was heavy intercity e-mail banter.) And this weekend, employees of both offices and their families were to attend the circus in Philadelphia.

Granted, not every employee goes to the events. But workers say the company's willingness to address differences has improved the relationship.

Chaney has also tried showing the staff the benefits of having two different perspectives on the same account. For a leading maker of athletic shoes and clothing, New York did a sweaty, gritty, black-and-white campaign, while Malvern chose something more colorful, centering on the fashion. Both have been presented to the prospective client.

Neil Baror, 23, an art director in New York, spent eight days in Malvern for the Martha Stewart project. His biggest adjustment was the food, he said. "I'd never had a fried meatball until I went to Malvern," he said.

But dining together did help creative-department people like Baror learn to get along with technical people like Bruce McMahon, a senior programmer. "We've become good friends," McMahon said. "Once they came down here, it was much better. We're a little more laid back here. They're kind of high-strung and tense."

McMahon is among the employees who have used the company's intranet to get to know his colleagues. When he wanted more Coca-Cola and less Pepsi in the office, he conducted a e-mail poll for both offices about drink preferences. The winner turned out to be vodka.

US Interactive's two offices are about to become three—a two-employee unit will open in Washington April 20, and a possible merger with a company in Los Angeles in the offing, interoffice communication has become a high priority.

"We originally thought we'd be this hot virtual company where everyone who had a laptop could be wherever they wanted, Smith said. "We thought technology could overpower human nature."

But nothing, he added, can replace face-to-face meetings and "sharing, joking, drinking, playing golf."

The New York Times, April 18, 1998
http://www.nytimes.com/library/financial/Sunday/041998earn-culture-clash.html

CRITICAL THINKING QUESTIONS

1. How could culture clashes influence business communication?
2. Aside from nationality, how could culture clashes occur?
3. How has technology influenced culture clashes?
4. What steps could be taken to reduce business communication culture clashes within an organization?

SHORT APPLICATION ASSIGNMENTS

1. In teams of three to five, or as a class, discuss your responses to the preceding critical thinking questions.
2. Prepare a one-page memo report (200–250 words) to your instructor in which you respond to the critical thinking questions and offer a final summary of the article. You will find a model one-page report on the Web site (nytimes.swcollege.com).
3. Write an executive summary (200–250 words). As an administrative assistant to a busy executive, you are expected to summarize selected articles and present important points. You will find a model executive summary on the Web site.
4. Summarize this article (100–125 words) for your company's newsletter. You will find a model newsletter article on the Web site.

BUILDING RESEARCH SKILLS

1. Investigate how differences in nationality or differences in lifestyle influence business communication. Write a three to five page report that summarizes your findings.
2. Using at least three other references (books, journal articles, newspaper stories, magazine stories or credible Web sites) write an 800- to 1,000-word essay addressing two of the preceding critical thinking questions.
3. Using at least three other references (books, journal articles, newspaper stories, magazine stories or credible Web sites) post an 800- to 1,000-word Web page addressing at least two of the preceding critical thinking questions.

CHAPTER 2

Changing Technology
and Business Communication

PREVIEW

While many believe that the Internet is the most profound business communication tool ever, others yawn. Similar to the printing press, postal service, the telegraph, telephone, telefax, computer, radio, and television, the Internet is simply the latest business communication technology. Internet proponents counter that the Internet will soon incorporate these older technologies. Regardless, a historical perspective helps frame the Internet's effects—good and bad—on current and future business communication.

In "Monopolies, Standards, Goons and You," Ashley Dunn uses the history of railroads, telephones and computers to underscore the importance of standards. Consider the controversy about PC's versus Mac's, or Office 97 versus Office 2000; standards influence business communication.

Standards play a critical role for a future business communication tool, the digital set-top box. John Markoff illustrates the importance of standards, as well as this new tool, in "Microsoft Hunts Its Whale, the Digital Set-Top Box."

History shows that any new technology has intended and unintended, as well as positive and negative, consequences. Carl S. Kaplan's "Writer Seeks Balance in Internet Power Shifts," describes a guardedly optimistic view of the Internet's impact on communication.

Source: Christine M. Thompson/CyberTimes

Monopolies, Standards, Goons and You

By Ashley Dunn

No one thinks much today about the width of American railroad tracks. It's just one of the obscure statistics of technology—like the aspect ratio of a television or the frequency of CD lasers—that only engineers care about much anymore.

But this simple figure—four feet, eight-and-a-half inches—played a significant role in the industrial history of the United States as one of the keys to the consolidation of the railroads in the 19th century. Part of this nation's industrial history was determined by a few inches. It could have been five feet, a standard widely adopted in the South that provided greater stability at high speeds. It could have been less than four feet, which was used in the West because it was cheaper to build and more appropriate for rough terrain.

But it wasn't, and on that single issue rested the fates of hundreds of companies contending for the rail market. By the late 19th century, the United States had almost entirely moved to a unified rail gauge.

Local rail companies were swallowed up by a handful of behemoths that became rich through their power to dictate rates. They dominated transportation like a cartel until the emergence of cars and planes.

The cartel that ruled the rails was the first model of the oppressive and arrogant mega-companies that would follow in the industrial age. But at the same time, their forging of a unified rail standard, helped spur the nation's western expansion and kept the industrial plants of the East well fed with raw materials from the hinterlands.

The development of the rail infrastructure in the United States is beautifully detailed in a book, *Emerging Infrastructures: The Growth of Railroads*, by Amy Friedlander, a senior writer for the Corporation for National Research Initiatives. It is significant that the corporation, a nonprofit group formed to investigate issues relevant to the construction of the National Information Infrastructure, found it worthwhile to look at the development of the railroads.

There is always a danger in drawing too much from the past, but many parts of the railroad story sound familiar to computer users. The rough outline of the story has been echoed in the rise of modern behemoths—AT&T in telephone service, IBM in computer systems and now, Microsoft in its domination of the desktop operating system market.

In each case, these companies created a type of infrastructure that required a high level of standardization—whether it was for moving freight, analog signals, hardware systems or desktop files. Those who controlled the standard, controlled the industry. These companies pressed their advantage to the maximum, further increasing their domination of the market.

All, in their time, were responding to calls from consumers, government and industry to provide unified solutions. They were the dictatorships of technology that we put in power. Microsoft is the only latest goon. But really, if it didn't exist, we would have had to invent it.

There is a progression to these companies' climb to power. While the standards they set brought stability to the development of technology, they inevitably become oppressive as well.

It is hard to imagine now, but just three or four years ago the great hue and cry from users was over the jumble of software that contended within our computers. Why couldn't programs all work in the same way? Why couldn't they look the same and exchange information with each other?

Microsoft responded with Windows 95, which brought a level of integration that finally satisfied part of the user hunger. Because of the complexity and instability of Windows, those products outside of Microsoft were perceived, perhaps incorrectly in some cases, as less integrated and compatible. The result was the fading of virtually all of Microsoft's software competitors.

Like rail gauge, Windows wasn't better than the Mac OS or Unix; it was simply more widely accepted in business, where IBM had blazed the trail.

While Microsoft's position now seems unassailable, it is inevitable that its dominant position will gradually fade, like all those companies before it. The reason is the conflict between the static nature of standards and the dynamic flow of technological development.

Windows 95 has become a gangling behemoth in its effort to preserve its primacy on the desktop. The program has DLLs, drivers and all sorts of other pieces of code strewn across your hard drive. It doesn't keep up with new products very well, and when the program does advance, it throws the industry into turmoil because of all the internal changes.

In short, Windows 95, after just a few short years, has become as oppressive as the great railroad companies. It has become an impediment to progress because of its complexity and effect on developers. The old complaints about the jumble of programs on our computers has now given way to constant moaning over the unstable dictatorship of Windows.

Some company will eventually rise to meet this market demand for greater simplicity and interoperability. And no doubt Windows will survive for many more years. But with the rough standardization of the desktop accomplished, the computer has already begun leaping to the next step of standardization, provided by TCP/IP, HTML and perhaps Java.

The difference with these three is not only that they are open standards but that they represent a slightly higher level of organization. The Net standards were created to provide an interoperable environment—one that provides a framework for many different standards to coexist.

Interoperability is one step up the ladder of social organization, involving more intricate connections between humans and machines. It is the difference between railroads and paved roads, which are designed to accommodate many different types of vehicles, including bicycles, motorcycles, cars, buses and trucks. In many ways, they are the democracies of machine societies.

It seems clear that we are moving toward a time of greater interoperability, and the job of regulators should be to foster interoperability while keeping Microsoft from wresting too much control over that evolving standard.

But even as various governments' battles with Microsoft heat up, another force is rising on the horizon. It's not too hard to see that the next step in machine organization is already shaping up—the bandwidth shortage. If there is one greater complaint among users than Windows problems, it is the horrible lag and slow speed of the Net. This issue has hampered the deployment of Java, the use of video and sound, and the development of high-level interactive programs like online games and collaborative applications.

A number of efforts, like Internet II, promise a type of segregated service, separate from the morass of the current Net. It seems conceivable that access will begin to split into prioritized services, where some packets are treated better than others—for a price, of course.

For the next generation, those who control the pipes, will determine the shape of the consumer market—and the cycle of consolidation, standardization and domination will begin again.

CyberTimes, The New York Times on the Web, November 12, 1997
http://www.nytimes.com/library/cyber/surf/111297mind.html

CRITICAL THINKING QUESTIONS

1. How do technology standards effect business communication?
2. How would standards influence purchasing business communication hardware or software?
3. How do organizations establish business communication standards?
4. How does interoperability relate to standards?
5. What new technology standard battlefronts will influence future business communication?

SHORT APPLICATION ASSIGNMENTS

1. In teams of three to five, or as a class, discuss your responses to the preceding critical thinking questions.
2. Prepare a one-page memo report (200–250 words) to your instructor in which you respond to the critical thinking questions and offer a final summary of the article. You will find a model one-page report on the Web site (nytimes.swcollege.com).

3. Write an executive summary (200–250 words). As an administrative assistant to a busy executive, you are expected to summarize selected articles and present important points. You will find a model executive summary on the Web site.
4. Summarize this article (100–125 words) for your company's newsletter. You will find a model newsletter article on the Web site.
5. In teams of three to five, or as a class, discuss the advantages and disadvantages of technology standards in business communication. Be sure to include specific hardware and software examples in your discussion. Your instructor may ask you to share your results in a five-minute presentation or one-page memo.
6. Prepare a one-page memo report (200–250 words) to your instructor in which you explain how to convert a Microsoft Word document to an earlier version of Microsoft Word.

BUILDING RESEARCH SKILLS

1. Search Microsoft's Web site and other Web resources to see what options are available for reading later versions of Word or Excel from an older version of Word or Excel. Your instructor may ask you to submit a three- to five-page guide or post a Web page explaining the options you found.
2. Using at least three other references (books, journal articles, newspaper stories, magazine stories or credible Web sites) write an 800- to 1,000-word essay addressing two of the preceding critical thinking questions.
3. Using at least three other references (books, journal articles, newspaper stories, magazine stories or credible Web sites) post an 800- to 1,000-word Web page addressing at least two of the preceding critical thinking questions.

Microsoft Hunts Its Whale, the Digital Set-Top Box

By John Markoff

Has Bill Gates become the Captain Ahab of the information age?

Gates' white whale remains an elusive digital set-top cable box that his company, Microsoft Corp., is hoping will re-create the personal computer industry by blending the PC, the Internet and the television set into a leviathan living-room entertainment and information machine.

It has been an obsession for more than six years for Gates, whose "Windows everywhere" software strategy has led the company to look to extend its Windows operating system monopoly into every cranny of the computing industry—from mighty mainframes to the computers embedded in cars.

Still, it is the tantalizing possibility of the computerized television set that has fixated Gates most, leading to the construction some years ago of a faux living-room laboratory in a building on Microsoft's office campus in Redmond, Wash.

Presumably, that is because the prospect of digital television—part PC, part boob tube—promises the greatest return on the company's research and development investment. Digital television holds out the Holy Grail: the intersection of the nation's most vibrant industries, including media, computing, entertainment and telecommunications.

Small wonder, then, that Microsoft agreed last week to invest $5 billion in AT&T, as part of that company's deal to add MediaOne Group, the cable television company, to its recently acquired Tele-Communications Inc. cable empire.

Television sets are in some 98 percent of American households, while personal computers are having trouble breaking the 50 percent threshold. Thus, a Windows operating system monopoly on the set-top box would dwarf the scale of the PC industry.

"The television is the 3,000-pound gorilla," said Nicholas Donatiello, president of Odyssey, a market research firm in San Francisco.

And yet, just as Captain Ahab's quest for Moby Dick led to a miserable outcome, there is no certainty that Microsoft's quest for the television set top will succeed.

As early as 1993, Microsoft proposed a joint venture with Time Warner Inc., AT&T and TCI called Cablesoft, in an effort to harness the cable and phone industries to the Microsoft Windows software operating system standard. Since then Gates has repeatedly tried to forge pacts with partners in those industries.

Though some have welcomed such overtures, like Comcast, the cable company in which Microsoft acquired a 11 percent stake a few years ago, others have held back. The laggards feared they would inevitably fall victim to the same forces that enabled Microsoft to reduce many PC hardware makers to mere purveyors of commodity goods.

But Microsoft's considerable financial heft has eroded most resistance. Besides the Comcast stake, Gates' investments in his pursuit of interactive digital TV have included WebTV, Time Warner's Road Runner, four European interactive cable television investments and, finally, last week's investment in AT&T.

In return for a $5 billion stake, AT&T has warily agreed to license a minimum of 5 million copies of Microsoft's Windows CE operating system and engage in several showcase tryouts of the software, the consumer-electronics version of Microsoft's industry-dominating Windows software for PC's.

The deal will ensure that Microsoft gets an inside track in the new interactive television industry, which after years of delay appears to be showing some signs of life.

Clearly Microsoft's chairman believes with great certainty that interactive digital television is the Next Big Thing. And yet just as Gates, the visionary, entirely missed the dawning of the Internet, there is growing evidence that rapid technology transitions are not predictable—let alone manipulable.

In pushing for multimillion-dollar test runs, Gates may be ignoring years of consumer indifference and outright interactive television failures like Time Warner's debacle in Orlando, Fla., a few years back—not to mention the rapid emergence of a range of alternative technologies for delivering Internet content that may quickly bypass the living room.

The risk to Gates is that the interactive television set, upon which he is betting most heavily, may prove a mirage that wastes billions of dollars of investment capital and Microsoft development efforts.

The offspring of a dream that stretches as far back as the 1970s, digital television has long been a Chimera pursued by high-technology executives— whether in the form of videotext, video on demand or, more recently, Internet via television.

The new hope is that while no one has been able to figure out the challenge of how to supply more than several channels of compelling programming for a television audience simultaneously, the World Wide Web would offer an easy solution.

Both AT&T and Microsoft envision that the DTC-5000, a set-top box due this fall from General Instrument, will serve as a choke point for all the digital information flowing into and out of the home.

The original vision of interactive cable has now stretched far beyond 500 channels to include telephone service, video on demand, stereo audio, video games and Internet access. As a result of this "all things to all people" impulse, the DTC-5000 has sometimes been derided as an information-age Cuisinart.

Indeed, the joke inside AT&T labs, where engineers are testing the box, is that DTC-5000 has so many connectors that the physical integrity of its back panel has been compromised. The prototypes include connections for cable, power, Ethernet and Firewire networks, Universal Serial Bus, telephony, audio, video, infrared, PCMCIA card, smart card and computer monitor.

While simpler and more compelling alternatives—ranging from the home PC to a growing array of wireless and hand-held computers and phones—offer a seemingly more convenient way to obtain Internet data, Gates has continued to pursue the parallels between the world of interactive digital television and the personal computer industry, and to re-create a dominant role for Microsoft. Indeed, forcing Windows CE on the cable industry has become a virtual religious crusade inside Microsoft's headquarters.

"This is a big frontier, and Bill is scared to death that it's going to pass him by," said a member of the AT&T team that negotiated the deal with Microsoft. As described by Microsoft's deal-maker and chief financial officer, Greg Maffei, the investment makes sense as a bet on the future of high-capacity—or broadband—telecommunications networks.

"There is finally a plan to go out and deploy something, and that's a great opportunity for us," Maffei said in a telephone interview Thursday, after the deal closed.

Microsoft executives argue that a business rationale now exists for interactive television—as opposed to the Orlando interactive television pilot that Time Warner started with great fanfare in 1994 only to unceremoniously shut it down in 1997.

"Deregulation is allowing a single supplier and pipe into the home to provide digital television, telephony and high-speed Internet access," said Hank Vigil, vice president for consumer strategy at Microsoft.

Yet, the crusade to bring E-commerce to the family-room sofa is probably no closer this week than before the arrival of last week's alliance between the software and the telecommunications industry giants.

In particular, AT&T will be competing with other technologies challenging cable as a means to deliver Internet data: fixed and cellular wireless telecommunications; the phone industry's digital subscriber line and interactive satellite systems from the Hughes Electronics subsidiary of General Motors.

Moreover, other technologies—including the PC, digital videocassette recorders from companies like Replay Networks Inc. and Tivo Inc., as well as a new generation of video game players from Sony, Sega and Nintendo—will all contribute to the accelerating fragmentation of the mass cable-television market.

AT&T may even become its own largest competitor, especially for providing consumers access to Internet electronic commerce. The company has quietly accelerated plans for a nationwide introduction of Internet-ready cellular phones, skipping 64 kilobits a second and going directly to 384 kilobits.

Such a network will be ideal for a new generation of Internet-compatible telephone-Web browsers now being shown by Nokia and Ericsson. Though a shift to mobile Web browsing would be warmly greeted by AT&T, it is likely to sharply limit the market for consumers willing to buy an expensive additional Internet account just to permit them to browse the Web on their TV.

And in the mobile and wireless world, Microsoft is already at a clear disadvantage competing with the cellular phone industry, which has shown little interest in a Microsoft Windows CE operating system.

Gates appears to have nearly infinite capital to invest in his dream, but there seems to be little to ensure that he will be able to enact his vision. That, of course, is the risk of being a visionary.

The New York Times, May 10, 1999
http://www.nytimes.com/library/tech/99/05/biztech/articles/10box.html

CRITICAL THINKING QUESTIONS

1. What makes more sense and why: a television that functions as a computer or a computer that functions as a television? Or, why do neither make sense?
2. How would a digital set-top box influence business communication?
3. Why has interactive television failed in the past?
4. What technology will win the battle to deliver Internet data to the home and office? Will one technology win at home while another wins at the office? Why?

SHORT APPLICATION ASSIGNMENTS

1. In teams of three to five, or as a class, discuss your responses to the preceding critical thinking questions.
2. Prepare a one-page memo report (200–250 words) to your instructor in which you respond to the critical thinking questions and offer a final summary of the article. You will find a model one-page report on the Web site (nytimes.swcollege.com).
3. Write an executive summary (200–250 words). As an administrative assistant to a busy executive, you are expected to summarize selected articles and present important points. You will find a model executive summary on the Web site.
4. Summarize this article (100–125 words) for your company's newsletter. You will find a model newsletter article on the Web site.
5. Phone or visit television and computer stores in your community to compare their interactive television or set-top box options. Your instructor may ask you to share your results in a five-minute presentation or one-page memo.
6. What options exist in your community to deliver Internet data to the home and office? Your instructor may ask you to share your results in a five-minute presentation or one-page memo.

BUILDING RESEARCH SKILLS

1. Phone or visit television and computer stores in your community to compare their interactive television or set-top box options. Your instructor may ask you to submit a three- to five-page guide or post a Web page explaining the options you found.

2. What options exist in your community to deliver Internet data to the home and office? Your instructor may ask you to submit a three- to five-page guide or post a Web page explaining the options you found.

3. Using at least three other references (books, journal articles, newspaper stories, magazine stories or credible Web sites) write an 800- to 1,000-word essay addressing two of the preceding critical thinking questions. Assume that this essay will be used as an internal reference for a corporation's Internet manual.

4. Using at least three other references (books, journal articles, newspaper stories, magazine stories or credible Web sites) post an 800- to 1,000-word Web page addressing at least two of the preceding critical thinking questions. Assume that this page will be posted on a corporate intranet.

Writer Seeks Balance in Internet Power Shifts

By Carl S. Kaplan

NEW YORK—Musicians make end-runs around record companies by putting their songs online for fans to download directly. "Day traders" buy and sell stocks without the help of brokers. Readers use filters to screen news, entertainment and even people.

There is a common thread running through these and similar Internet developments, according to Andrew L. Shapiro, a writer and lawyer. What's going on is a potential—and in some cases actual—radical shift in power, as individuals use technology to wrest control over information and resources away from large institutions like the Government, corporations and the media.

Some observers might think this trend is a positive one because it promotes personal freedom and democratic values. And Shapiro, too, counts himself as a "guarded optimist" about the Internet. But in *The Control Revolution*, his nuanced and provocative new book that examines core legal and policy issues presented by the Internet age, Shapiro does something most cyber-pundits don't do. He spends a lot of time depicting how the revolution he admires can too easily go wrong.

"This can all backfire," Shapiro, 31, said in a recent interview at a Soho restaurant.

When people use technology to customize their lives to the hilt, and in the process eliminate middlemen like editors, politicians and local retailers, there is a danger that they can become too narrow-minded and tune out from the wider world, Shapiro said.

The upshot is that cyberspace, justly lauded for its diversity and wealth of information, can breed self-imposed ignorance and over-involvement in virtual communities, at the expense of active citizenship and strong, real-world local communities, he said.

"There's got to be a balance between individual power and the obligations of the individual to something greater—a sense of community, democratic values," said Shapiro.

An outgoing man with curly red hair and freckles, Shapiro enthusiastically chops the air with his hands when he speaks about the Internet. He also has a quality of unshakeable self-confidence, possibly a gift from his years at Brown University and Yale Law School.

No stranger to cyberspace legal debates, Shapiro started writing about the Internet for *The Nation* magazine while he was still a law student. After clerking for a judge in the Federal Appeals Court for the Second Circuit in Manhattan, Shapiro hooked up with the Century Foundation (formerly the Twentieth Century Fund), which sponsored what became his new book, published this month in conjunction with PublicAffairs, a New York publisher. He has also worked at other foundations, serving as director of the Aspen Institute's Internet Policy Project and as a fellow at the Brennan Center at New York University Law School.

Most notably, Shapiro was one of the founders of Technorealism, a short-lived movement launched in March 1998 by 12 writers and editors. The group sought to stake out a pragmatic middle ground in the Internet policy wars between dewy-eyed utopianism and a disdainful rejection of technology.

But some critics lambasted the group as peddlers of obvious platitudes. Steven Levy, writing in *Newsweek*, dubbed the movement's founding statement "vapid" and "muddled." Slate's Michael Kinsley was less charitable.

Shapiro brushes away the memory. "I think we learned a lesson in how to initiate a public dialogue," he said. "People thought we had written a manifesto, but all we did was try to initiate a debate." He added that his new book, in part, is his personal attempt to be more specific about Internet issues, problems and solutions.

After setting forth his thesis that technology can shift control to individuals, Shapiro explores two caveats. One is the ongoing, counterrevolutionary effort by governments and corporations to grab back control of information. This can be seen in certain practices of the Microsoft Corp. that are the subject of the government's antitrust trial, or the effort by some book and music publishers to prevent copying of information without a digital key. The second hitch is that individual power can be misused, a phenomenon he calls "oversteer," as when a driver tries too hard to control a car and spins off the road.

The last part of Shapiro's book contains some solutions to the problems he addresses. He calls, for example, for government-mandated "fair hacking" laws to support a user's right to make a "fair use" copy of a protected work. He would also like to see a requirement that gatekeepers like America Online and Microsoft create a space called a "public net"—similar to the public access channels on cable systems—where marginalized speakers can have their say.

The solutions Shapiro provides may carry a whiff of the seminar room, but he defends them as practical and necessary. He said that he is not opposed to having government regulate aspects of the Internet to achieve fairness and democratic values.

Lawrence Lessig, who taught Shapiro in a seminar on cyberspace law at Yale and now teaches at Harvard, called Shapiro's book "a great mapping of the subtle issues that usually get rolled over. Reading it, you get a sense of someone taking you into every corner of the problem very quickly."

But Lessig added that Shapiro, at the end of the day, is "a little more optimistic than I am." For one thing, the shift in control toward individuals has not yet stabilized, he said. In addition, even if people achieve more control over information, there's no guarantee they will exercise it to achieve power. "This is the bovine principle—tiny fences control large animals," he said.

CyberTimes, The New York Times on the Web, June 18, 1999
http://www.nytimes.com/library/tech/99/06/cyber/cyberlaw/18law.html

CRITICAL THINKING QUESTIONS

1. What are the advantages, and disadvantages, of the shift in power, as individuals use technology to wrest control over information and resources away from large institutions like the Government, corporations and the media?
2. How does this shift in power effect business communication?
3. How does technology shift control of information to individuals?
4. How are governments and corporations fighting this shift?
5. What future changes in information control do you envision occurring? How will these future changes affect business communication?

SHORT APPLICATION ASSIGNMENTS

1. In teams of three to five, or as a class, discuss your responses to the preceding critical thinking questions.
2. Prepare a one-page memo report (200–250 words) to your instructor in which you respond to the critical thinking questions and offer a final summary of the article. You will find a model one-page report on the Web site (nytimes.swcollege.com).
3. Write an executive summary (200–250 words). As an administrative assistant to a busy executive, you are expected to summarize selected articles and present important points. You will find a model executive summary on the Web site.
4. Summarize this article (100–125 words) for your company's newsletter. You will find a model newsletter article on the Web site.

BUILDING RESEARCH SKILLS

1. Using at least three other references (books, journal articles, newspaper stories, magazine stories or credible Web sites) write an 800- to 1,000-word essay addressing two of the preceding critical thinking questions. Assume that this essay is a background document for a corporation's marketing plan.
2. Using at least three other references (books, journal articles, newspaper stories, magazine stories or credible Web sites) post an 800- to 1,000-word Web page addressing at least two of the preceding critical thinking questions. Assume that this page is a background document for a corporation's marketing plan.

CHAPTER 3

Legal and Ethical Issues Influencing Business Communication

PREVIEW

Business communication has always had shades of gray. Some legal and ethical issues are simply not black and white. Far from clarifying the issues, today's technologies add another layer of gray. Digital communication and information is easy to create, store and replicate, yet surprisingly hard to control.

Two of today's biggest digital business communication issues are privacy and appropriate use. Who owns the rights to personal information? Who has the rights to, and how should organizations monitor, personal communication? Furthermore, what communication guidelines, if any, should organizations establish?

Given today's business communication's tenacity to survive, and multiply, organizations are rapidly establishing procedures to manage these digital records. Jeffrey L. Seglin explores how companies are tackling this tricky issue in "You've Got Mail. You're Being Watched.", while Pamela Mendels' "E-Mail Misuse a Growing University Concern," illustrates a disturbing university trend. Denise Caruso tackles another disturbing trend, one that has been around for decades. Her "Exploiting—and Protecting—Personal Information," investigates the conflict over who controls personal data.

Source: Christine M. Thompson/CyberTimes

You've Got Mail. You're Being Watched.

By Jeffrey L. Seglin

It was tragic," recalled Mary Beth Heying, a principal at Edward Jones & Company, the brokerage firm in St. Louis. In April, an employee had complained to the human resources department after receiving an e-mail containing inappropriate material, meaning off-color jokes, pornography and so on. "We investigated and found that a large number of associates were involved" in distributing such messages, Ms. Heying said. Depending on "the egregiousness of their involvement," she said, the company dismissed 19, warned 41 and allowed 1 to resign.

The company has a "very clear" written policy on e-mail, Ms. Heying said. Some 2,700 of its 17,000 employees have e-mail or Internet access at work (none of the brokers do, because written communication is heavily regulated in the brokerage industry), and each of the 2,700 was given a copy of the policy when receiving e-mail access, Ms. Heying said.

An American Management Association survey this year found that 27 percent of companies do what Edward Jones does—monitor internal e-mail—up from 20.2 percent in 1998. In the vast majority of cases, employees are informed of the surveillance.

There is little dispute that companies have both the power and the legal right to monitor e-mail sent on the company network on company time. But there are conflicting ethical imperatives at work when managers consider a monitoring policy: on the one hand, to avoid unwarranted intrusions into employees' privacy; on the other, to keep unchecked circulation of off-color jokes and other inappropriate material from creating a hostile atmosphere.

Allan A. Kennedy, a management consultant and co-author of *The New Corporate Cultures* (Perseus, 1999), starts from the premise that "companies that monitor e-mail traffic or use the power of modern technology to act as Big Brother to the employees are dehumanizing the work environment." Still, he sees a need for policing e-mail, given how it can expose a company to litigation. He says the best approach is to let workers frame the policy.

"An employee-based e-mail monitoring system would not be as disrespectful," he said. "It would be from one employee to another, saying 'We don't want to work in an environment where this kind of thing goes on.' It'd be equivalent to the kind of natural monitoring that would have gone on around the water cooler."

In reality, though, monitoring is rarely continuous; far more often it is used only when a company has someone or something to investigate—when, as at Edward Jones, an employee complains about a particular message. Indeed,

Laura P. Hartman, a professor of business ethics at the University of Wisconsin, thinks the threat of monitoring may be seen as a strong-enough deterrent that companies can spare themselves from much actual monitoring.

Employers are naturally uneasy about unmasking inappropriate e-mail and dismissing offenders.

But invasion of privacy isn't the root of the unease; the distress of firing is. Most managers dread having to do something so painful to the person across the desk. "We have a zero tolerance policy with regard to inappropriate e-mail, and people know that," Ms. Heying said. "Does that mean we didn't feel badly about 20 associates? Oh, by all means, we do."

E-mail takes companies into new ethical territory, as they struggle with controlling a technology so utterly different from other communications tools. Unlike a phone call or hallway conversation, e-mail leaves an audit trail that can pinpoint the abuser. But unlike a paper memo, e-mail moves at lightning speed, both in delivery and in composition, often with little reflection or second thought. It will probably be awhile before there is corporate consensus on the fairest balance between privacy and protection.

Until then, the responsibility to do the right thing falls upon employees, who can use common sense as a guide.

If an employee's passion for e-mail privacy is born of a desire not to have the boss find out he's been placing bids all day for vintage comic books in an online auction, chances are he already knows he shouldn't be doing that at work.

In this new high-technology world, a remarkably old-fashioned rule of thumb applies: Don't do what you wouldn't want to be caught doing.

The New York Times, July 18, 1999
http://www.nytimes.com/library/tech/99/07/biztech/articles/18ethics.html

CRITICAL THINKING QUESTIONS

1. Should an organization monitor employee e-mail? Why, or why not?
2. What is the best way to frame an organization's e-mail policy that protects both employees' privacy and the organization's working atmosphere?
3. What makes e-mail different from other forms of business communication?
4. What basic guidelines should an organization establish regarding use of its e-mail?
5. Would it be fair to fire an employee for e-mailing a joke to another employee? Why, or why not?

SHORT APPLICATION ASSIGNMENTS

1. In teams of three to five, or as a class, discuss your responses to the preceding critical thinking questions.

2. Prepare a one-page memo report (200–250 words) to your instructor in which you respond to the critical thinking questions and offer a final summary of the article. You will find a model one-page report on the Web site (nytimes.swcollege.com).

3. Write an executive summary (200–250 words). As an administrative assistant to a busy executive, you are expected to summarize selected articles and present important points. You will find a model executive summary on the Web site.

4. Summarize this article (100–125 words) for your company's newsletter. You will find a model newsletter article on the Web site.

5. In teams of three to five, or as a class, draft an e-mail monitoring policy for your school or organization. Your instructor may ask you to share your results in a five-minute presentation or one-page memo.

BUILDING RESEARCH SKILLS

1. Individually or in teams, draft an e-mail monitoring policy for your school or organization. Your instructor may give you a sample organization as well as ask you to submit a three- to five-page policy handbook or post a Web page, along with a letter of transmittal explaining the project.

2. Using at least three other references (books, journal articles, newspaper stories, magazine stories or credible Web sites) write an 800- to 1,000-word essay addressing two of the preceding critical thinking questions. Assume that this essay will be used as an internal reference for a corporation's Internet manual.

3. Using at least three other references (books, journal articles, newspaper stories, magazine stories or credible Web sites) post an 800- to 1,000-word Web page addressing at least two of the preceding critical thinking questions. Assume that this page will be posted on a corporate intranet.

E-Mail Misuse a Growing University Concern

By Pamela Mendels

As he does most mornings right after he awakens, John C. Wu walked groggily to the laptop in his dorm room at Stanford University the Saturday of Memorial Day weekend to check his e-mail.

Wu, a sophomore, expected to find the usual fare: notes with details on assignments from teaching assistants, messages from friends, comments to class e-mail lists.

This time, however, what he found was a shock: a two-paragraph vulgarity-filled message spewing racial slurs and lashing out at black and Hispanic students. "These were words I have never heard people speak," said Wu, a computer science major. "It was terrible."

And it was widespread.

The message was received by about 25,000 students, professors and staff members at the Palo Alto, Calif., university before computer technicians stopped its distribution. The mailing provoked a series of letters to the editor of the campus newspaper as well as a special meeting between university officials and students, and is now the subject of an investigation by a high-tech crime unit at the Santa Clara County district attorney's office. In an open letter to the Stanford community, the president of the university, Gerhard Casper, denounced the "appalling epithets" in the note and said the views expressed were "personally offensive to me, and, I trust, will be rejected by the entire community."

What is perhaps most surprising about the incident, however, is that it is not unique. A number of universities in recent years have been shaken by incidents in which an e-mail message containing offensive and bigoted material got circulated, in some cases widely, on campus.

"The universities are extremely concerned about this kind of hate-mongering behavior," said Virginia E. Rezmierski, a computer policy official at the University of Michigan and director of a project to study computer misdeeds in institutions of higher education. "We are very concerned that the technology be used as positively as possible to create community, not destroy it."

Statistics on the phenomenon are hard to find. Universities, like corporations and other institutions, are loathe to publicize incidents involving computer misuse, partly out of fear of bad publicity, partly out of concern about disclosing their internal computer security measures. But Majorie Hodges Shaw, co-director of Cornell University's Computer Policy and Law Program, estimates that there are one to two such incidents per semester across the United States.

And some people believe universities should brace themselves for more.

Michael J. Gennaco, an assistant U.S. attorney in Los Angeles and a prosecutor in two cases involving racist e-mail messages at universities, says he is currently investigating several more incidents. "It's an increasing problem," he said. "As people have better access to e-mail, there will be people who will abuse it. It's particularly true at universities, where e-mail has become the mode of choice for communicating between people."

Sometimes, the identity of the sender is known. That was the case at Cornell in 1995, when four college freshman sent an e-mail message to friends containing what they viewed as a joke offering 75 reasons why women should not have freedom of speech. The message was quickly distributed to others who failed to find its contents amusing, resulting in a campus outcry and national publicity.

In other incidents, the identity of the sender is masked. That is what happened several years ago at the University of Michigan, according to Rezmierski. A racially charged message, with the return address of a university undergraduate, was sent to numerous people on and off campus. The address turned out to be forged; the message was not sent by the student whose name appeared as the sender. But recipients had no way of knowing this and bombarded the purported sender with angry responses. The true author of the message has not been found, Rezmierski said.

At Stanford, too, the identity of the sender is so far unknown. The note contained the return address of a Stanford student, but in his letter, Casper said campus police did not believe the alleged source was the author and that a university computer security specialist had determined that the message had not been posted from the student's account.

How universities deal with the incidents vary with each episode. When the message involves a forgery or unauthorized intrusion into the university's computer system, its sender could be liable under various computer crime laws or university acceptable use policies.

But when such violations have not occurred, the matter gets trickier, because of free speech concerns. "It is difficult to address words through a disciplinary process unless they reach the level of harassment," said Hodges Shaw.

It is yet to be determined what Stanford policies, if any, the contents of the message breached, said Kathy O'Toole, a Stanford spokeswoman. In his letter, Casper said that once the sender was identified, officials would "use all the means available to us to take appropriate action."

On its Web site, the university has posted an extensive computer use policy, dated June 1997, which bans activities including violations of software copyright and attempts to crash the computer system. It also forbids the use of e-mail to send "fraudulent, harassing, obscene, threatening, or other messages that are a violation of applicable federal, state or other law or University policy."

For Karen K. Wang, a Stanford freshman who also received the message, a suitable response to the incident is one that emphasizes the exchange of ideas characteristic of an academic setting. "The only solution," she said, "is a lot more discussion on campus attitudes toward race."

CyberTimes, The New York Times on the Web, June 9, 1999
http://www.nytimes.com/library/tech/99/06/cyber/education/09education.html

CRITICAL THINKING QUESTIONS

1. Should universities provide students with e-mail accounts or point them toward free e-mail accounts such as HotMail or Yahoo! Mail?
2. Should "free speech" apply to students' use of e-mail? Why, or why not?
3. What could be done to combat e-mail misuse at universities?
4. How should universities discipline students that misuse e-mail?

SHORT APPLICATION ASSIGNMENTS

1. In teams of three to five, or as a class, discuss your responses to the preceding critical thinking questions.
2. Prepare a one-page memo report (200–250 words) to your instructor in which you respond to the critical thinking questions and offer a final summary of the article. You will find a model one-page report on the Web site (nytimes.swcollege.com).
3. Write an executive summary (200–250 words). As an administrative assistant to a busy executive, you are expected to summarize selected articles and present important points. You will find a model executive summary on the Web site.
4. Summarize this article (100–125 words) for your company's newsletter. You will find a model newsletter article on the Web site.
5. In teams of three to five, or as a class, draft a plan to combat e-mail misuse at your university. Your instructor may ask you to share your results in a five-minute presentation or one-page memo.

BUILDING RESEARCH SKILLS

1. Individually or in teams, draft an e-mail monitoring policy for your school or organization. Your instructor may give you a sample organization as well as ask you to submit a three- to five-page policy handbook or post a Web page, along with a letter of transmittal explaining the project.
2. Using at least three other references (books, journal articles, newspaper stories, magazine stories or credible Web sites) write an 800- to 1,000-word essay addressing two of the preceding critical thinking questions. Assume that this essay will be used as an internal reference for a corporation's Internet manual.
3. Using at least three other references (books, journal articles, newspaper stories, magazine stories or credible Web sites) post an 800- to 1,000-word Web page addressing at least two of the preceding critical thinking questions. Assume that this page will be posted on a corporate intranet.

Exploiting—and Protecting—
Personal Information

By Denise Caruso

For the last few weeks, the data privacy battle has been waged with such fury that privacy advocates have not known whether to cry, cheer or simply assume the fetal position.

Personal privacy—the disposition of all those pieces of information that computers hold about each of us—has been debated in the electronic world for almost two decades. Although the issues are complex, the bottom lines have always been pretty clearly drawn.

People and companies that sell personal data want to be able to collect and distribute it pretty much with abandon, and they fight like cornered weasels at even the suggestion of government regulation.

Yet, most people online—87 percent in a 1997 Georgia Tech survey—want "complete control" over their personal data. And if they feel violated by data collectors, they often scream bloody murder.

In 1991, for example, Lotus Corp. was forced to cancel shipments of Marketplace, a CD-ROM data base, after receiving thousands of angry e-pistles from people who took grievous offense at the data base's content: the names, addresses, income levels, numbers of children and other data for every household in the United States.

More recently, privacy advocates wrested a partial victory from Intel Corp., after the company announced that its new Pentium III chips contained embedded electronic serial numbers for authenticating documents, e-mail and copyrighted material. Watchdogs warned that the numbers could be used to identify a computer to prying software, or to allow companies or agencies to track a person's movements across the Internet.

Intel refused to remove the number, but agreed to provide software that allows computer makers to hide it behind a digital fig leaf, software that some say has already been compromised.

And the California Legislature, often a bellwether for technology issues, is considering more than a dozen privacy laws, including one that would restrict the collection and disclosure of personal information by government, business or nonprofit organizations. It specifically includes information gathered via Internet sites.

Still, plenty of others are rushing to cash in on the data gold rush.

Privacy advocates were extremely cranky after discovering that Florida, South Carolina and Colorado were selling residents' driver's license information to a New Hampshire-based company, Image Data LLC.

They were even more outraged to discover that the Secret Service had financed another private company's efforts to develop a national data base of driver's license photographs.

And in the most telling testament yet to the commercial value of personal data in the Internet economy, a start-up called Free PC announced that it would provide a free Internet connection and a free Compaq computer to anyone willing to "apply" by answering a detailed questionnaire and then accepting constant bombardment by advertisers based on the personal profile created from the questionnaire.

Rich Le Furgy, chairman of the Internet Advertising Bureau, an industry group, said that advertisers haven't even begun to tap the Internet's potential. They are now investigating how to aim promotions at individual consumers based on their online behavior: Vendors want to co-market products in much the same way that convenience stores did after discovering, for example, that people who buy beer also often buy diapers at the same time.

Not exactly music to the ears of a privacy-sensitive consumer. Obviously, online advertising organizations find themselves straddling a very pointy fence between companies that pay for advertising and customers who are subjected to that advertising. The constituencies have very different viewpoints, and finding a solution palatable to both is not a task for the squeamish.

For example, Le Furgy said, "it would be a beautiful thing" for consumers to control their personal data—especially if it meant avoiding legislation and regulation.

"Privacy is an enabler of commerce," he said. If consumers can get money for their personal information and still control it, "they'll be much more willing to provide it."

In fact, a new breed of Internet company is already making a business of that concept.

These companies, known as infomediaries—a term coined by John Hagel, co-author of *Net Worth: Shaping Markets When Customers Make the Rules* (Harvard Business School Press, 1999)—will step in and help consumers regain control of their personal data.

For a price, of course.

A recent Wired News feature predicts that an up and coming pack of these entrepreneurs will "cut the consumer in" on the deal when information about them is bought and sold. Infomediaries keep a percentage for themselves for providing the security mechanisms by which consumers can control exactly who buys their personal data and for what purpose.

But some privacy advocates would eliminate even the infomediary and pass laws granting consumers not just civil rights to their privacy, but property rights to their private data, ending the free-market eminent domain that data marketers have exploited for decades.

Citing a Virginia law that forbids the use of anyone's name or likeness without permission, Ram Avrahami, a business consultant, unsuccessfully sued *U.S. News & World Report* in 1996 for selling his name to another magazine. At the time, Avrahami's opponents ridiculed him for suing over 8 cents, which is what the magazine had paid for his name.

"The point is this: It's 8 cents for me, for you, for 100 million other Americans, which becomes big money," said Avrahami, who has since become a leading advocate of private data ownership. "Think of it this way: Free PC proves that our personal information is worth hundreds of dollars. Now, who should get those dollars, if not us?"

The New York Times, March 1, 1999
http://www.nytimes.com/library/tech/99/03/biztech/articles/01digi.html

CRITICAL THINKING QUESTIONS

1. What regulations, if any, should control the sale of personal data?
2. Should individuals have "complete control" over their personal data? Why, or why not?
3. What are the various ways that companies collect and store personal data?
4. How could personal data improve business communication?
5. What future trends in collecting personal data do you envision occurring? How will these future trends affect business communication?

SHORT APPLICATION ASSIGNMENTS

1. In teams of three to five, or as a class, discuss your responses to the preceding critical thinking questions.
2. Prepare a one-page memo report (200–250 words) to your instructor in which you respond to the critical thinking questions and offer a final summary of the article. You will find a model one-page report on the Web site (nytimes.swcollege.com).
3. Write an executive summary (200–250 words). As an administrative assistant to a busy executive, you are expected to summarize selected articles and present important points. You will find a model executive summary on the Web site.
4. Summarize this article (100–125 words) for your company's newsletter. You will find a model newsletter article on the Web site.
5. In teams of three to five, or as a class, discuss the TRUSTe and Council of Better Business Bureaus' BBBOnLine privacy guidelines. Your instructor may ask you to share your results in a five-minute presentation or one-page memo.
6. Fill out the necessary forms, and investigate the privacy policy for a free e-mail account with Yahoo! or HotMail. What did you think of the questions asked? Their privacy policy? Your instructor may ask you to share your results in a five-minute presentation or one-page memo.

BUILDING RESEARCH SKILLS

1. Review the information on and various Web sites linked from the *New York Times on the Web* privacy information page. Your instructor may ask you to submit a three- to five-page summary or post a Web page explaining the information you found.
2. In teams of three to five, or individually, draft privacy guidelines for your school or company. Your instructor may ask you to submit a three- to five-page policy handbook, along with a letter of transmittal explaining the project. You may use the TRUSTe, Council of Better Business Bureaus' BBBOnLine or other online sources as sample privacy guidelines.
3. Using at least three other references (books, journal articles, newspaper stories, magazine stories or credible Web sites) write an 800- to 1,000-word essay addressing two of the preceding critical thinking questions.
4. Using at least three other references (books, journal articles, newspaper stories, magazine stories or credible Web sites) post an 800- to 1,000-word Web page addressing at least two of the preceding critical thinking questions.

Business Communication Tools—
Old and New

PREVIEW

Businesses have a quiver of new internal and external communication tools today. Although shooting these powerful arrows can be easy, hitting the target is not. Sometimes simple technologies, like pen on paper, work better.

Depending on the circumstances, are handwritten notes more apropos than electronic ones? Is handwriting a lost art? Lisa Napoli's "Penmanship in the Digital Age," examines these questions. Although e-mailing notes and other messages is surprisingly simple, most businesses are unprepared and understaffed for responding to their customer's e-mails. Pamela LiCalzi O'Connell, in "We Got Your E-Mail; Just Don't Expect a Reply," dispels the "one-to-one" communication myth.

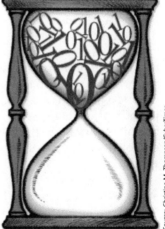

Internet chat, another new communication tool, offers one-to-one communication. But unlike e-mail, which is asynchronous, chat is synchronous e-mail. Similar to talking on the phone versus leaving a voice mail message, chat happens in real time while e-mail has a time delay. Michel Marriott explores how organizations and individuals chat—effectively and ineffectively—in "The Blossoming of Internet Chat."

Source: Christine M. Thompson/CyberTimes

Penmanship in the Digital Age

By Lisa Napoli

A friend called to thank me for the condolence note I'd sent after her father died.

Isn't it interesting," she said, kindly. "We wouldn't think of sending a condolence e-mail. It's one of the few places where a handwritten note still seems necessary."

I felt a bit embarrassed, because I had had a fleeting thought to send an e-mail when I'd heard the news. What it offered in immediacy, though, it lacked in taste. I instantly ruled it out as inappropriate, and headed for the file cabinet and the box of personal note cards I keep for thank you notes and instances like this.

Then, I took out a pen and wrote, deliberately and thoughtfully, scratch-ing out the words as if I was dressing my handwriting in its Sunday solemn best.

After talking with my friend a few days later, I wondered: will mine be the last generation to feel that personal notes carry a certain meaning? And what are the circumstances, in this digital age, in which handwriting is proper—as opposed to an electronically transmitted sentiment? I'd written about love in the age of e-mail for Valentine's Day; if e-mailed love missives were now culturally acceptable, and condolence notes were not, what between love and death was left?

Just as I was deliberating, I glanced at the note pad where I record phone messages and ideas, and I couldn't decipher something I'd written down the day before.

That's when I realized that this debate I was having within myself wasn't as much about protocol, as it was about penmanship.

For as long as I can remember, I have loved the feeling of pen on paper, controlling a flow of ideas—the stroke of the pen as extension of my thoughts. My junior high school friend Liz and I used to plant ourselves on the porches of one of our houses in Brooklyn after school, sprawled on chairs, and scrawling on notepads. Harriet-the-Spy-esque diarists, this was our adolescent idea of a good time.

We'd sit in silence for hours, writing, drinking hot tea, and then occasionally stop to share our thoughts. It wasn't what we wrote as much as that we wrote it.

I remember the individuality of our respective styles. Mine was straight and cartoon-like, and Liz's was a bit more tilted and sophisticated. Both were still distinctly precise, teen-age; neither one of us wrote in cursive. Perhaps that was an unconscious way of rebelling against the convention expected of us at that age; perhaps it was just our personalities.

Separated in college, I missed Liz but still felt connected to her, because she'd write me long missives in her handwriting. I imagined her sitting with another friend, someplace quiet, and musing on paper in the way only she could. Reading the missives was like spending an afternoon on the porch with her.

Liz doesn't write to me any more (the phone is easier) but when I see her handwriting, usually on notes on her fridge in her house, I feel like I'm 13 again.

Two of my family's most prized artifacts hang in my mother's study. When I was 22 months old, my father sat me down and asked me to talk. He wrote down every word I said in his distinctive bold, block print style, and framed the finished piece like artwork.

"Mom mom, dad dad, dog, cat, beach, ice cream" and so on reads the artwork, ending with the word, "Macy's."

He did the same with my little brother when he was 22 months old. Mine is in red magic marker, and James's is in blue, and only in recent years has the paper on which our father recorded our vocabularies begun to yellow behind the glass and slim black frames. His handwriting, like Liz's and mine, has evolved over the years, but is still clearly his. Seeing it is almost a better clue to what he must have been like as a young man, a proud new father.

There are dozens of photographs to remind me of what I looked like as a child, but my spoken words on paper are the only record of my toddler voice.

I used to love to help laying out the newsletter for my dorm at Hampshire College, Merrill House, in the early '80's. It's called Fred, and it's distributed in the bathrooms, with such important information as the dining hall menu and vacuum cleaner availability at the house office.

The most elaborate part of the production of this literal house "organ" was the Letraset, the rub-on letters I'd been introduced to by my dad years before. Letraset was my first experience with this thing called fonts, and type sizes, and the delicate beauty of the letters could also be maddening if you missed a corner, or leaned on a character too soon or forcefully.

But now that I think about it, Letraset was mystifying, too, because it was my second encounter with manipulating type other than by my own hand. (The first would have been lettered blocks.) Even before I'd learned the type-writer keyboard, my dad had me rubbing off letters for flyers he made, and sitting several years later at college, lining up headlines, evoked a strange memory. A psychologist might say that I had a deep-seated disdain for something that usurped my lovely print style.

By my late teens, in college, my lovely print style had dissipated to "doctor-style" scribble. Thoughts became too urgent, and time too precious, to be deliberate.

Those were the days when typing a letter was still seen as verboten, impersonal, rude. I started to type my letters back in college to spare the recipient the deciphering, but I'd always sign with a flourish and at least several hand-written P.S. addenda—as if to apologize for the formality with an extreme informality.

Now, if I get any sort of personal letter in the mail, I rip it open instantly with delight. That anyone would take the time or make the effort makes it more important than any other correspondence.

But letters are few and far between these days, and even the flow of post-cards, society's simplest vestige of hand-inked mail, seems to have dissipated this summer.

For years, I had a mental catalogue of the handwriting of my closest friends and family, the way you know the voices of the people closest to you without introduction. I know the facts of the lives of my newer friends, and their stylistic marks and quirks, but, for the most part, I don't know their handwriting.

It struck me recently that of all the intimate details I know about a person who has become important to me, I had never seen evidence of his penmanship. Communication was not one of our problems; in fact, sometimes it was consuming. But none of our communiqués included handwritten notes.

Afraid to seem intrusive, or questioning of our intimacy, I asked, in a casual e-mail, for a sample. It must have seemed frivolous or unnecessary, or perhaps my offhanded request got lost in the shuffle of the electronic in-box.

Or perhaps to my friend, as to many people, there is no deeper meaning to handwriting in this digital age. Writing a card to someone who had suffered a loss has made me realize how intimate, how dear it has become to me—even and especially in non-urgent circumstance.

Today, I'm going to take a piece of paper and go sit outside, and write a letter—not just a note—and force myself to think without a keyboard, to remember how it feels. The exercise will be a cathartic experiment, and it won't be altruistic: I'm hoping that whomever I choose to receive my letter will write back.

CyberTimes, New York Times on the Web, October 8, 1997
http://www.nytimes.com/library/cyber/week/100897penmanship.html

CRITICAL THINKING QUESTIONS

1. What are the circumstances, in this digital age, in which handwriting is proper—as opposed to an electronically transmitted sentiment?
2. When would it be appropriate to send business communication via the telephone, fax, surface mail, courier or e-mail?
3. Are electronic postcards such as those found on Blue Mountain Arts or American Greetings, a business communication tool? Why, or why not?

SHORT APPLICATION ASSIGNMENTS

1. In teams of three to five, or as a class, discuss your responses to the preceding critical thinking questions.

2. Prepare a one-page memo report (200–250 words) to your instructor in which you respond to the critical thinking questions and offer a final summary of the article. You will find a model one-page report on the Web site (nytimes.swcollege.com).
3. Write an executive summary (200–250 words). As an administrative assistant to a busy executive, you are expected to summarize selected articles and present important points. You will find a model executive summary on the Web site.
4. Summarize this article (100–125 words) for your company's newsletter. You will find a model newsletter article on the Web site.
5. Query one family member, friend and fellow employee or student about the appropriate medium for different types of business communication. Your instructor may ask you to share your results in a five-minute presentation or one-page memo.

BUILDING RESEARCH SKILLS

1. Using at least three other references (books, journal articles, newspaper stories, magazine stories or credible Web sites) write an 800- to 1,000-word essay addressing two of the preceding critical thinking questions.
2. Using at least three other references (books, journal articles, newspaper stories, magazine stories or credible Web sites) post an 800- to 1,000-word Web page addressing at least two of the preceding critical thinking questions.

We Got Your E-Mail;
Just Don't Expect a Reply

By Pamela LiCalzi O'Connell

Some dare call it electronic commerce.

A major consumer products company logged 264,000 telephone calls to its customer service center in a recent month and handled 225,000 in what it considered satisfactory fashion—a "close" rate of 85 percent.

And during the same period, the center's service representative received about 20,000 customer e-mail messages via the Internet. Just 2,000—a measly 10 percent—received attentive replies, and some not for several weeks. (This data was shared on the condition that the company not be identified.)

Say hello to the Web as black hole.

E-commerce? One-to-one communication? The promise of these buzzwords is belied by simple reality: many companies, even those with a seemingly sophisticated presence on the World Wide Web, continue to treat customer e-mail as second-class communication.

Anecdotal evidence and some limited market research confirm that unless a company is a Web-based business to start with, like the online bookseller Amazon.com the organization is likely to lack the tools and policies to handle the inflow of messages from its Web site.

"When companies go on the Web they tend to immediately get overwhelmed by messages," said Donna Hoffman, an associate professor at the Owen Graduate School of Management at Vanderbilt University. "But some still don't see handling this e-mail as one of the most important customer service jobs. They haven't created the proper policies or allocated the funds."

Professor Hoffman, the director of an influential research program that studies the marketing implications of commercializing the Web, finds it disturbing that her own frequent messages to commercial sites almost never result in a response. Web users may lose trust in the medium if their experience is similar, she said.

According to a survey earlier this year by First Data Investor Services Group, which supplies transaction services to mutual fund companies, 82 percent of the mutual fund Web sites it tracks advertise themselves as offering customer service via e-mail. Yet when First Data tried to measure how long it took each site to respond to e-mail, it found that about 30 percent of customer messages never got any response.

A reporter's unscientific spot check of the consumer-contact e-mail addresses on the Web sites of two dozen well-known, consumer-focused corporations did not fare much better: only seven of the sites responded in less than 24 hours, and five of the companies never replied.

One of the companies that did reply—though it took a couple of days—was Nike, a company known for its marketing prowess. Even though it is not a big online retailer, Nike sees sufficient value in the more than 2,000 e-mail messages its site receives daily that the company has devised extensive procedures for handling the volume.

"At some forward-looking companies there is a realization that you don't get to hear from customers often—that you should treasure it and find a way to deal with every e-mail," said Martha Rogers, a partner at Peppers & Rogers Group in Stamford, Conn., a consulting firm that focuses on "one to one" marketing.

A recent report by Forrester Research was based on interviews with 37 companies that Forrester selected as especially intent on customer e-mail. Even among those companies, which average 500 incoming e-mails a day, dealing with the deluge can be confusing, with responsibility split among departments. And most of the companies sampled still manually route messages—despite being aware of automation tools that would speed the process.

One such technology for automating customer e-mail is Echomail from General Interactive Inc. in Cambridge, Mass. Echomail, uses natural-language and "discourse analysis" software to parse messages in an attempt to classify them as, say, a complaint, a sales lead or an investor inquiry. In some cases automated responses may be sent, but most messages are typically routed to customer-service agents.

Echomail users include Nike, I.B.M., AT&T, Lycos, J. C. Penney and Allstate.

"Before someone puts in our system," said V. A. Shiva, president and chief executive of General Interactive, "we ask them, 'Do you value e-mail? Do you have policies and processes for handling this inflow? Whose responsibility is this mail, marketing or customer service or someone else? What happens to a message, for instance, if it hasn't been read in five days?'"

Shiva added that the slow adoption of systems to handle incoming e-mail had "a lot to do with technology but also with process and elevation of consciousness—even politics going on within companies."

Cost is probably a consideration, too, since such systems often sell for $200,000 or more, according to Forrester.

Shiva and other industry executives say that companies could often create smarter customer-contact pages on their Web sites that would greatly simplify e-mail management. An increasing number of corporate sites ask—or even require—customers to complete a Web form rather than send a free-form message.

Even though some might find the templates intimidating or off-putting, the consumers who do proceed will be providing information that makes it easier for the company to route and respond to the message.

At the leading edge of managing customer e-mail are companies that have trained their phone agents to handle e-mail, too, treating it as simply another type of customer communication.

"A science has built up around handling 800-number calls after all these years, but on the Web we are only recently seeing those disciplines applied to handling customer e-mail," said Don Morrison, executive vice president of Chordiant Software Inc. in Palo Alto, Calif., a provider of customer-interaction technology.

Still, Morrison points out the some messages, like those involving order confirmations or complex instructions, are better handled by e-mail than phone calls.

In fact, the discount stockbroker Charles Schwab is actively trying to increase the percentage of customer queries handled by e-mail rather than by phone, said Paul Raskin, director of Schwab's electronic brokerage services unit. E-mail now accounts for one-third of customer inquiries to the unit, up from one-tenth two years ago.

As an example of a consumer-focused company that has increasingly moved its business on line, Schwab was quick to recognize the value of customer messages.

"We actively promote e-mail as a customer-service channel," and electronic brokerage services receives up to 15,000 electronic messages a week, Raskin said. About a quarter of the 300 service agents that Raskin has working at any one time are devoted to handling e-mail.

Schwab, like most companies that deal with consumer e-mail, is reluctant to send out automated responses.

With automated responses the human aspect is lost, Professor Hoffman said, "and that goes against the whole idea of trying to create the appearance of a personal relationship" on line.

Even companies that do use boilerplate replies tend to reserve them for only the most common questions—as Nike, does, for example, with queries about the location of the nearest retailer.

One significant exception is Lycos, the Web-searching service. With only two customer-service representatives, Lycos uses Echomail's automated response capability to handle the majority of its incoming messages—most of which have to do with the listings and navigation on its site.

Lycos's experience with Echomail's parsing capabilities has been positive, with 80 percent or more of the responses being appropriate replies to the queries, said Adam Gross, a senior customer-service representative for the company. Among the 20 percent of inapplicable responses was one to a reporter's spot check. A question asking how to use Lycos to count the number of sites on the Web that are linked to a specific home page was answered with, "We appreciate your desire to place a link to Lycos," and instructions on how to link a home page to the service.

The timing of automated responses can be a sensitive issue. Although the system is able to reply automatically within five minutes, Gross has set it to respond at a more human pace—within 12 hours. Why?

"If the response comes right away, the customer may discount it as just a machine talking," Gross said. "Even if the answer is full and correct, they'll view it with disdain."

The New York Times, July 6, 1998
http://www.nytimes.com/library/tech/98/07/biztech/articles/06mail.html

CRITICAL THINKING QUESTIONS

1. Should an organization encourage their Web site visitors to contact them via e-mail? Why, or why not?
2. When would it be appropriate for an organization to use automated e-mail responses?
3. Is telephone or e-mail the more effective way for an organization to communicate with customers? Why?
4. What priority should be given to customer e-mails? How soon should it be answered? By whom?

SHORT APPLICATION ASSIGNMENTS

1. In teams of three to five, or as a class, discuss your responses to the preceding critical thinking questions.
2. Prepare a one-page memo report (200–250 words) to your instructor in which you respond to the critical thinking questions and offer a final summary of the article. You will find a model one-page report on the Web site (nytimes.swcollege.com).
3. Write an executive summary (200–250 words). As an administrative assistant to a busy executive, you are expected to summarize selected articles and present important points. You will find a model executive summary on the Web site.
4. Summarize this article (100–125 words) for your company's newsletter. You will find a model newsletter article on the Web site.
5. In teams of three to five, or as a class, draft an e-mail response policy for your school or organization's Web site. Your instructor may ask you to share your results in a five-minute presentation or one-page memo.
6. In teams of three to five, e-mail a relevant question to an organization. How long did it take the organization to respond? Did the organization answer your question? Your instructor may ask you to share your results in a five-minute presentation or one-page memo.

BUILDING RESEARCH SKILLS

1. Individually or in teams, draft an e-mail response policy for your school or organization's Web site. Your instructor may give you a sample organization as well as ask you to submit a three- to five-page policy handbook or post a Web page, along with a letter of transmittal explaining the project.

2. Using at least three other references (books, journal articles, newspaper stories, magazine stories or credible Web sites) write an 800- to 1,000-word essay addressing two of the preceding critical thinking questions. Assume that this essay will be used as an internal reference for a corporation's Internet manual.

3. Using at least three other references (books, journal articles, newspaper stories, magazine stories or credible Web sites) post an 800- to 1,000-word Web page addressing at least two of the preceding critical thinking questions. Assume that this page will be posted on a corporate intranet.

The Blossoming of Internet Chat
Moving from Gossip, Flirting and Worse to Education, Consumer Service and Even More Gossip

By Michel Marriott

Since the first time someone went online and thought to type in a question like "What are you wearing?" to an unseen stranger in cyberspace, computer chat has had a somewhat shady reputation.

At its best, chat has been a way to waste time, the equivalent of being a teenager on the telephone but with a dozen chums at once. At worst, chat has been about cybersex, and lots of chat rooms have been seedy locations, virtual back alleys where pedophiles and sexual predators lurked.

But chat is changing, maturing, diversifying.

"Until now, chat was something my aunt used to talk to her friends about making doll-house clothing," said Marty Focazio, director of strategic services at Spiral Media, an Internet development company based in New York. "But I use it basically for fast, tactical communication, whether I'm in or out of the office."

Chat is being used in business, education and consumer service. It is turning out to be a way to promote television and movie stars and to provide a forum for authors to talk to their readers. It is also being renamed "real-time customer interaction" and labeled an "Internet collaboration tool."

"Right now, chat is the easiest and most reliable way to communicate over the Internet in real time," said James P. Tito, president and chief executive of Eshare Technologies, a major provider of chat technology to companies like Merrill Lynch, 1-800-Flowers, Mail Boxes Etc. and AT&T Worldnet Services. The company, based in Commack, N.Y., also provides chat services to 100 universities, including Yale and Cornell, so they can stretch physical classrooms into virtual ones by offering distance education.

"It's a way that most people can use the Internet," Tito said. "You don't need any specific equipment or special browser or special plug-ins."

Tito estimates that of the 107 million people who use the Internet worldwide, at least 40 million to 50 million of them use chat in some fashion, including the more recent innovations of one-on-one chat pioneered by America Online's Buddy List and Instant Messenger systems. AOL, which, with 12 million users, is the largest online service in the United States, recently found that its users spent 19 percent of their time in online chat rooms, 2 percentage points more than the time they spent combing the Internet.

Doug Hirsch, a senior producer at Yahoo!, described chat as a ubiquitous "everyman's tool" that "can be used in any way anyone would want to use it."

Yahoo!, an Internet media company, itself schedules at least 100 chat events a month, Hirsch said. At The Globe, an Internet site that encourages its users to build online communities, about 30 percent of its more than five million users chatted on line, said Stephan Paternot, the company's president and co-founder.

Not that chat has gone completely sober and serious. Consider this recent exchange with Gena Lee Nolin, the actress who plays the "Baywatch" bad gal Neely Capshaw.

> *Dandeanie asks: Does it scare you knowing that people out there on the Net obsess over you?*
>
> *Nolin: Do they obsess over me? Oh, that flatters me! I didn't know they obsessed over me, though. Wow.*
>
> *CoolKiss84 asks: I want to be an actress. How do I get an agent and a manager?*
>
> *Nolin: Well, where do you live? If you live in L.A. or N.Y. (you should be based there) you need to get photos taken and have some sort of acting experience.*

The conversation was made possible by Big Star Entertainment, an online movie store that arranges regularly scheduled chats in a partnership with Yahoo!.

Nolin only had to talk on the telephone from her home in Los Angeles while Big Star's staff read questions to her and had her answers typed and dispatched into cyberspace. In all, some 5,500 questions buzzed across the Internet to Nolin in the 30 minutes before the chat officially began and during the hour it lasted. She answered as many as she could, or cared to (she ignored questions about whether her figure had been surgically enhanced).

Computer chat, practically born with the Internet almost 30 years ago, is a simple, sometimes bumpy, means of immediate online communication in which people type live messages over computer networks. People can chat one–on–one or in groups. The responses are live also, so a conversation among several people can make about as much sense as the babble when a group of people in a room all talk at once.

One way to talk on line is to enter a chat room, or forum, by following the directions at America Online or Microsoft Networks to one of their chat rooms or by logging on directly to a chat site on a Web page like Big Star's or the one offered by Ivillage: The Women's Network. Conversations there are wide-ranging, touching on topics like health, careers, relationships and rearing children.

Another way to chat is through instant messages. AOL members have long been able to send instant messages to other members that flash on the screen—

SITE-SEEING: CHAT ROOMS

So there's all this chatting on the Internet and you want to join the big conversation. Where do you begin?

An easy way to get started is to enter the chat rooms of online service providers like America Online and the Microsoft Network. These chat rooms are simple to use and are organized in categories like arts, entertainment, news, sports, finance and romance.

On the Web, major Internet information services like Yahoo! and Excite offer a broad range of free chat rooms. One of the largest chat offerings is on Internet Relay Chat, though connecting requires special software like MIRC, a shareware program that can be downloaded at www.geocities.com/~mirc/. But caution is warranted. Some of the hundreds of I.R.C. chat rooms are sexually oriented and not subject to the rules against vulgarity that most online services have.

---

if the recipient is on line—no matter what that person is doing. And other programs like Ding make it possible to send instant messages on the Web. As with many other aspects of the Internet, what was once a means for people to connect with one another has become a commercial tool.

Chat is certainly a natural way to promote entertainment figures.

"Everybody is doing chat now," said Jerry Shandrew, the publicist for Nolin and a number of other stars and supermodels he has nudged to chat on line. "It's the Internet, so you can reach an audience all over the world, and you can put people directly in touch with someone. That's exciting and personal."

A spokeswoman for America Online, Wendy Goldberg, agreed, noting that a chat in May with some of the stars of ABC's popular Friday night sitcoms had drawn 117,000 people, AOL's largest chat audience.

But chat is by no means limited to Hollywood. Almost at the same time as the chat with ABC stars, a collection of international scientists and business leaders met in a chat forum to discuss biotechnology and its implications. This month, a California computer game maker is starting a chat room for toddlers, while all sorts of groups, like computer manufacturers and the Internal Revenue Service, are exploring chat as a way to improve customer service while lowering costs.

"You hear a lot of times that people don't communicate anymore," Goldberg said. "But people are communicating a lot more now."

She said her 78-year-old aunt and her mother, who lives in Massachusetts, frequently used AOL's Instant Messenger service, which opens a chat window between two computers linked to AOL.

Sometimes, Goldberg said with a chuckle, her mother will go on line and notice that Goldberg is on line and working late in AOL's corporate office in Reston, Va. Using chat technology, Goldberg's mother sends her daughter instant messages that urge her not to work so hard and to get to bed.

David Phipps, a lawyer in a Los Angeles suburb who is a volunteer host for a technology chat room on the Microsoft Network, said chat helped make sense out of the chaos that often rules the Internet. Computer chat makes communicating with many people almost as easy as communicating with one.

"Most people can't talk and listen at the same time because our own voices drown out all others," Phipps said.

"In an Internet chat room, many people can talk at once. The computer sorts it all out and displays everyone's statements in order."

Well, most of the time. While the speed of computers and Internet connections have surged in recent years, some longtime computer users like Laura Balsam, a computer consultant in New York, are not overly impressed with chat technology.

"In general," she said, "chat rooms are so slow. You type something and five minutes later, someone responds to you."

On the other hand, Balsam said she liked instant chat, those message windows that, unlike open chat rooms, link only those who know one another.

"It's like walking down the street and sometimes running into a friend," she said. "It's a spontaneous kind of thing."

It is precisely that kind of comfort with chat that Richard Dym, vice president of marketing for Tribal Voice of Scotts Valley, Calif., is counting on as he tries to broaden chat's reach into more homes, offices and classrooms with Pow Wow, he said.

Pow Wow, he explained, is a software program that lets users create their own chat rooms. Room can be entered only with keys, which can be given to up to 800 people, far extending the usual chat-room limit of 25. The program, like Ding by Activerse of Austin, Tex., offers instant messaging and the ability for users to see quickly if users in the lists they create are actually on line.

Pow Wow and Ding also offer Internet telephony, the ability to transmit instant voice messages over the Internet. In fact, Dym said, just as chat is expanding, its end may be in sight. He said full Internet telephony would overtake and mostly replace text-based chat in a few years.

Many disagree with Dym's forecast, especially online chatters who say they enjoy a level of anonymity that text-only chat provides them.

"Text-based chat is probably always going to be there in some shape or form," said Tito, Eshare Technologies' president. "No matter what you do, it is very difficult for 50 people to actually talk all at the same time."

Randal Vaughn, a professor of information systems at Baylor University in Waco, Tex., said he used Pow Wow's chat system—without telephony—to extend his reach to his students, who are extremely computer literate.

He said his three undergraduate classes tended to be large, each with about 50 students.

Dr. Vaughn said computer chat had helped him reach more students, extending his office hours by allowing him to meet with many of them on line.

He recalled how one of his students had recently encountered a problem while working as a Web developer 10 miles off campus. By using chat, the student and the professor found a solution together.

Another advantage of chat, Dr. Vaughn said, is that students using a crowded computer laboratory can confer with him in his office without leaving their seats and losing their turns with the computers.

"It's all voluntary," he said, adding that his classroom chats were also popular.

Many businesses are also turning to chat. Eshare Technology is setting up chat-based customer service for 1-800-Flowers that is expected to begin later this month.

Tito said it would permit people to use their Internet connections to not only communicate in real time with a company representative but also to see and choose flower arrangements on line.

On the lighter side, many Internet multiplayer game services use chat rooms as meeting places for players to choose sides, discuss strategies or simply brag about their prowess. Multitude, a computer game company in Burlingame, Calif., is testing Fire Team, an Internet collaborative game that is played in squads in which players are linked through voice chat so they can speak and listen to one another through headsets as they coordinate their play.

And this month, Gizmo Gypsies, a children's computer game company in Santa Clara, Calif., is starting the Little Wizard Activity Center, which features an Internet chat room for children 3 to 8 years old.

The baby chatters will appear as cartoon bugs with their names attached to them. The child simply clicks on a picture of a gesture along the screen's lower edge and the bug waves, jumps, dances or squawks, among other things, in bugspeak.

"At the moment, the kids just go into rooms and experience other bugs and the kids," said Mike Hayes, the company's chief executive. "We also want to provide them with the opportunity to maybe get into a room with a grandparent or mom or dad."

Hayes said the bug chat room, called Bugville, would break new ground and help children prepare for communicating on the Internet. "They are getting the benefit of starting to understand that there are other people in this world," Hayes said. "And that they are totally unpredictable."

The New York Times, July 2, 1998
http://www.nytimes.com/library/tech/98/07/circuits/articles/02chat.html

CRITICAL THINKING QUESTIONS

1. How could chat be used for business communication?
2. Do chat's advantages as a business communication tool outweigh it's disadvantages? Why, or why not?
3. How does chat compare with other forms of business communication such as telephone, fax, reports, letters, memos or e-mail?
4. What would be ineffective uses of chat for business communication?
5. For effective business communication, what limits, if any, should be placed on the number of people chatting simultaneously?

SHORT APPLICATION ASSIGNMENTS

1. In teams of three to five, or as a class, discuss your responses to the preceding critical thinking questions.
2. Prepare a one-page memo report (200–250 words) to your instructor in which you respond to the critical thinking questions and offer a final summary of the article. You will find a model one-page report on the Web site (nytimes.swcollege.com).
3. Write an executive summary (200–250 words). As an administrative assistant to a busy executive, you are expected to summarize selected articles and present important points. You will find a model executive summary on the Web site.
4. Summarize this article (100–125 words) for your company's newsletter. You will find a model newsletter article on the Web site.
5. In teams of three to five, or as a class, experiment with chatting. Your instructor may ask you to share your results in a five-minute presentation or one-page memo.

BUILDING RESEARCH SKILLS

1. Individually or in teams, draft a plan to effectively use chat for business communication at your university or organization. Your instructor may give you a sample organization as well as ask you to submit a three- to five-page policy plan or post a Web page, along with a letter of transmittal explaining the project.
2. Using at least three other references (books, journal articles, newspaper stories, magazine stories or credible Web sites) write an 800- to 1,000-word essay addressing two of the preceding critical thinking questions. Assume that this essay is a background document for a corporation's marketing plan.
3. Using at least three other references (books, journal articles, newspaper stories, magazine stories or credible Web sites) post an 800- to 1,000-word Web page addressing at least two of the preceding critical thinking questions. Assume that this page is a background document for a corporation's marketing plan.

Internet Business Communication Skills

PREVIEW

The Internet is a powerful, albeit double-edged, business communication tool. The advantages of e-mail—speed, ease of use and broad reach—slice both ways. In a few keystrokes, experienced and especially inexperienced, users inadvertently launch blundering e-mail missives to the masses. The Web contains hundreds of millions of pages, yet finding the right page with reliable information—if it exists at all—takes time and can cause frustration.

As e-mail use increases and evolves, e-mail etiquette becomes a mandatory business communication skill. In "Tracking the Evolution of E-Mail Etiquette," Katie Hafner explores e-mail's modern manners.

The last two articles examine harvesting information from another Internet communication tool, the World Wide Web. Matt Lake investigates the mechanics behind, and better use of, popular search sites in "Desperately Seeking Susan OR Suzie NOT Sushi." And like any other information source, notes Tina Kelley in "Whales in the Minnesota River?", you should question a Web site's credibility and reliability.

Source: Christine M. Thompson/CyberTimes

Tracking the Evolution of E-Mail Etiquette

By Katie Hafner

As technologies evolve, so do the manners surrounding their use.

Take the telephone. Alexander Graham Bell considered "Ahoy! Ahoy!" the correct way to answer a telephone. Allen Koenigsberg, a classics professor at Brooklyn College, said it took until 1880, three years after commercial phone service was introduced in the United States, for the jauntier "Hello" to win out over Bell's choice and other contenders, like the impossibly proper "What is wanted?" and a confused "Is anybody there?"

The etiquette of e-mail, the ever more popular flow of messages from computer to computer via the Internet, is still in its formative stages. But that doesn't mean nobody is thinking about it. Dozens of e-mail etiquette primers can be found on the Web. And many companies now distribute guidelines on e-mail usage to employees, although the guidelines tend to focus on the contents of messages.

A few conventions are widely accepted. By now, most electronic correspondents know that informal salutations and sign-offs are perfectly acceptable but that typing in all capital letters, which comes across as virtual shouting, is not. Regular e-mailers know that they must watch what they write because e-mail is not necessarily private and that chain letters are not just considered tacky but are banned from many corporate e-mail systems.

As the flood of e-mail has grown, it has become clear that people are seeing far more of other people's unedited thoughts than ever before, both at work and outside it. That is partly because e-mail is so much easier to use than paper correspondence, as are the features that allow people to reply to, send, forward and redirect—and occasionally misdirect—a message.

But people are usually left to their own devices when it comes to use of Redirect, Forward, Cc (carbon), Bcc (blind carbon) and other features that appear in the e-mail header, the part of the message that serves as a virtual envelope and contains the time, date and addressing information. In the last few years, people have developed personal styles on the use of these functions that are highly idiosyncratic yet sometimes carefully considered.

E-mail has been around since the mid-60's, when it was used on computer time-sharing systems, and it has offered carbon, reply and forward features since the early 70's.

The kind of e-mail sent from machine to machine first cropped up in the 1970's, and its use has been growing ever since.

According to the International Data Corporation, a market research company, roughly 2.1 billion e-mail messages are sent each day in the United States, nearly double the volume at the end of 1997. That number is expected to reach 8 billion by 2002.

E-mail mores and faux pas matter most in workplaces where a growing reliance on e-mail for discussions and decisions means that entire days can pass without a single face-to-face meeting. E-mail use at work now rivals, and in some cases eclipses, the use of the telephone. One misdirected message, or an ill-tempered e-mail sent when emotions are heated, can threaten a career.

People who have been using e-mail for a long time have learned to be judicious in using the Cc feature.

Harry J. Saal, a philanthropist and entrepreneur in Silicon Valley, began using e-mail more than 20 years ago, when he was a manager at International Business Machines and used the company's internal e-mail system. "One of the things I've realized is how very much my usage of Cc and Bcc has changed over the years," Dr. Saal said.

Dr. Saal once used the Cc feature "as a kind of not very effective bludgeon to bug someone to do something, somehow involving someone else as an observer in the process, maybe their boss," he said. Now he rarely uses Cc because he considers it unnecessary. "About the only times I use Cc these days is for trying to set up a joint meeting with more than two people," he said.

Even relative beginners—which includes most people—can be highly sophisticated in their thinking about their e-mail. "We all use Cc for the right and wrong reasons," said Martha Feingold, director of talent at ZDTV in San Francisco. "We use it to praise ourselves," she said, or for self-protection. She said some people used Cc as a way to show off, putting people in the Cc field not because they need to be there but because they want to advertise the acquaintance.

Many people who regularly send e-mail—jokes, say, or a newsletter—to a large number of people hide their recipient lists to avoid clutter. Some e-mail programs have an option for hiding recipients in the Cc field, but people do it different ways, depending on the software used. One of the more conspicuous slips of the finger took place in the summer of 1997, when John Perry Barlow, who is known to socialize with celebrities both in and out of the digerati, accidentally forgot to hide the recipients on his "BarlowFriendz" list when sending one of his periodic dispatches. So several hundred private e-mail addresses, including those of John F. Kennedy Jr. and the actress Darryl Hannah, landed in the In box of each person on the list.

Shortly after discovering the gaffe, Barlow sent out a lengthy, self-effacing apology to the people on the list. "I felt terrible about it," he said.

Dave Winer, author of a newsletter about the computer industry, came up with a more creative solution for masking his recipient list. When the Davenet newsletter goes out, he uses a random number generator to select 11 names and put them in the To field of the e-mail header—each person in the group therefore finds out the e-mail addresses of the other people in that group. The process continues 90 more times, until the newsletter has been sent to all of the 1,000 recipients. "It makes it more interesting," Winer said. "There's this sense of connection they get." Winer said he had seen e-mail discussions break out on several occasions among the 11 recipients in a group.

Frequent e-mail users draw a sharp distinction between being included in the To field and being included in the Cc field. As they see it, to be in the To field is to be part of the discussion at hand. "I feel obliged to get into the fray if I'm part of the To field," said Daphne Kis, president and chief executive of Edventure Holdings, an information services and venture-capital firm in New York. Recipients included in the Cc field, however, often consider themselves bystanders who have no particular obligation to participate.

Bcc—the feature for sending blind copies, hidden from the view of the recipient in the To field—is more controversial. "Bcc should be illegal," said Guy Hoffman, chief executive of Deja News, a company in Austin, Tex., that archives Usenet newsgroups. "It's like recording a call without informing the other party."

Mark Erickson, vice president for culinary development at Digital Chef, an online retailer of specialty foods and cookware in St. Helena, Calif., agrees. "The whole concept of 'blind copy' gives me a feeling of inner-office politics that aren't on the up and up," he said. "I have never used it in all my years of business."

Some people ease a guilty conscience by forwarding a copy of a piece of e-mail to someone without telling the recipient of the original. The effect is the same: someone receives a message without the original recipient knowing that has happened.

Ellen Spertus, an assistant professor of computer science at Mills College in Oakland, Calif., said she used Bcc occasionally but also forwarded copies of messages separately. "I consider it more honest to forward the mail separately than to do Bcc," she said.

Others say the Bcc function is nothing to be ashamed of. At Michael Kaminer Public Relations in New York, Bcc's fly around the office nearly as often as out-in-the-open e-mail. "Bcc's the best thing in the world," said Michael Kaminer, the company's president. "At my company we like to let every single person know everything about every single account I work on. It's a nice way for me to keep everyone here up to date.

"You don't want everyone to know you're copying 15 people on a message. A note to someone seems a lot less personal when there are 10 other names in the Cc field."

Some people don't use Bcc because they don't trust it. Allison Thomas, a management consultant in Studio City, Calif., simply does not trust the e-mail program to send a blind carbon copy that is truly blind. "Everyone's probably gotten burned somewhere along the line," she said. Instead, like those who feel guilty about sending an actual blind copy, Ms. Thomas sends copies of e-mail to third parties after the fact.

The Reply function may seem perfectly straightforward, but it, too, has its drawbacks. Most e-mail programs, upon receiving this command, include the text of the previous message—as well as all the messages that preceded it. The result can be a message that's a mile long with history. Dr. Saal said he took great pains to winnow his messages as an exchange continued, retaining only the most relevant text.

A different problem, at the other end of the spectrum, arises when an electronic dialogue loses its context entirely. "I get pieces of mail responding to something I wrote a week earlier that just says, 'It's a deal!' and I have no idea what they're talking about," Dr. Saal said.

Then there's the Reply to All function, which can bring in all too many people on a heated discussion. "I discovered the potential for hostility in e-mail is huge, and very disruptive for managing groups of people," said Stuart Gannes, vice president for Internet applications at the Menlo Studio at AT&T Labs in Menlo Park, Calif. "People got on their high horse and became very preachy toward each other. These incredibly hostile arguments that were copied to everyone would erupt. You're challenging someone in public. These things are like little wildfires."

To avoid such situations, Gannes has developed a rule for the group he manages. "If you want to directly confront somebody, don't reply to all," he said. "Just reply to the person who disturbed you."

A stickier predicament arises from confusion over the Redirect and Forward functions. People often choose Redirect (found in Eudora but not many other e-mail programs) for a message without realizing that it leaves the original sender's name in the From field. That means that when recipients reply to the message, the reply makes a beeline for the original sender, not for the person who redirected the message. When someone uses Forward to send you a message, on the other hand, you can choose Reply to send a message back to the person who forwarded the e-mail message, not to the original sender.

"Redirect is implemented in a terrible way, leading to terrible faux pas situations," said Einar Stefferud, an Internet management consultant in Huntington Beach, Calif. Stefferud, who used some of the original e-mail systems in the 1970's, does not use his Redirect feature.

The Forward function comes with its own set of perils. "You forward an entire message to someone without necessarily thinking about what's at the bottom," said Kaminer, the Bcc fan. "You might have said that person is a schmuck lower in the e-mail and forgotten to take it out."

Misdirected e-mail can get messy. Nearly everyone has a story to tell of embarrassment caused by a stray electronic arrow.

Stacey Wells, a reporter at The Oakland Tribune in Oakland, Calif., recalled a nearly disastrous mistake that occurred when the Newspaper Guild she was helping to organize was pursuing a contract with management. When Ms. Wells sent out a confidential piece of e-mail outlining the group's strategy, it accidentally ended up in the computer of a high-level executive whose name stood dangerously close to that of the intended recipient in an electronic address book. "We were nailed," Ms. Wells said. Naturally, the organizers were forced to change their strategy.

Now, Ms. Wells said, "I double-read all my e-mail, and everyone it's addressed to. And for anything that's the least bit personal, I call them."

"With a computer, it's so easy to hit the wrong button," said Robert Bender, a senior editor at Simon & Schuster in New York. "I don't know how they avoid this kind of thing at the White House and the Pentagon. Tell the Chinese prime minister to go jump in a lake and the next thing you know, troops are lining up at the border."

Enter the Escape key, which can pull a message back from the brink just as it is being sent—if you're quick enough. "The Escape key has saved my life on several occasions," Kaminer said. "But you have to have a really fast draw to get it in time."

The New York Times, December 10, 1998
http://www.nytimes.com/library/tech/98/12/circuits/articles/10mail.html

CRITICAL THINKING QUESTIONS

1. When addressing e-mail, what are appropriate and inappropriate use of the To, Cc and Bcc field? Why?
2. When composing e-mail, what grammatical conventions should be followed? Why?
3. Under what circumstances is it appropriate to forward or redirect e-mail? Why?
4. Name three specific widely accepted e-mail etiquette norms. Why are these so widely accepted?

SHORT APPLICATION ASSIGNMENTS

1. In teams of three to five, or as a class, discuss your responses to the preceding critical thinking questions.
2. Prepare a one-page memo report (200–250 words) to your instructor in which you respond to the critical thinking questions and offer a final summary of the article. You will find a model one-page report on the Web site (nytimes.swcollege.com).
3. Write an executive summary (200–250 words). As an administrative assistant to a busy executive, you are expected to summarize selected articles and present important points. You will find a model executive summary on the Web site.
4. Summarize this article (100–125 words) for your company's newsletter. You will find a model newsletter article on the Web site.

BUILDING RESEARCH SKILLS

1. In teams of three to five, or individually, draft an e-mail policy for your school. Your instructor may ask you to submit a three- to five-page policy handbook, along with a letter of transmittal explaining the project.

2. In teams of three to five, or individually, draft a computer use (games, e-mail, Web surfing, etc.) policy for your school or company. Your instructor may ask you to submit a three- to five-page policy handbook, along with a letter of transmittal explaining the project.

3. Using at least three other references (books, journal articles, newspaper stories, magazine stories or credible Web sites) write an 800- to 1,000-word essay addressing two of the preceding critical thinking questions.

4. Using at least three other references (books, journal articles, newspaper stories, magazine stories or credible Web sites) post an 800- to 1,000-word Web page addressing at least two of the preceding critical thinking questions.

Desperately Seeking Susan
OR Suzie NOT Sushi

By Matt Lake

If the World Wide Web ever adopted a theme song, it could do worse than picking "I Still Haven't Found What I'm Looking For." Searching the Web is the most popular online activity—and often the most frustrating. In June, more than half of the top 10 most-visited domains were Web search sites, according to an Internet metering service, Media Metrix. But how many of the people visiting those sites found what they were looking for right away?

Not most, according to Karin Rex, whose Pennsylvania-based company Computer Ease conducts Internet search classes. "Most people type in words and get a bazillion hits," Ms. Rex said. "Some of the ones on the first page may pertain to what they're looking for, but most of them won't."

On the surface, it ought to be simple. You're looking for Lincoln's Gettysburg Address, you enter those three words, and assuming it's somewhere on the Internet (and that's a pretty safe assumption), the search site gives you a list of relevant Web pages. Right? Not so, Ms. Rex said.

"You'll get sites about the Lincoln Continental and vacations in Gettysburg, and real-estate sites listing addresses," she said, "but often, nothing about Lincoln's Gettysburg Address."

Danny Sullivan, editor of the Search Engine Watch newsletter, agrees. His publication and Web site monitor the world of Web searching, and despite improvements over the past two years, he said, he still sees problems.

"They've gotten better, faster and easier to use, but search engines have got a long way to go," Sullivan said. "They're poor for people who are doing really basic searches. Enter 'Disney' or 'travel,' and it's a crapshoot whether they'll get the Disney site or any good travel sites."

One search site could provide 10 top results of pure gold, while another serves up either nothing or dross. Why is there a difference in results? Because there are three basic components of all search engines, and while there is often a lot of overlap, no two engines are exactly the same. One element is the index of Web sites or Web pages that your search roots through; each search site collects its information and updates its database differently. Each site's search function works differently, too, and the order in which the results are sorted is usually based on a proprietary algorithm that no company would be willing to share.

To make things harder, search sites generally do not do a good job of explaining how they work. Few people understand, for example, that Yahoo! is fundamentally different from search sites like Hotbot, AltaVista and Infoseek.

Yahoo! is not really a search engine but rather a Web directory, compiled by humans who classify Web sites under headings. The others are Web search engines, which use software agents called crawlers or spiders to index the contents of individual Web pages, then follow links to other pages.

Web directories like Yahoo! and Web search engines may look the same, but each type of site is good for finding different types of information.

The first step in creating more effective searches is picking the right search site for the job. "If people are doing a general search," Sullivan said, "they should start off at Yahoo! or a Yahoo!-like directory like Snap or Look Smart." A directory-style search provides two ways to research broad topics: dive through a list of broad topics by clicking on the appropriate links or fill out a search box to find listings.

But directory searches are less effective when looking for specific information—things like the author of a book, the complete text of the Declaration of Independence or research on drug treatments for a medical condition. For this kind of information, search engines like Hotbot and AltaVista are the way to go. Because they search an index of keywords drawn by spiders from millions of Web pages, the chances are greater that they will find obscure terms in obscure Web pages.

There's a third kind of search site, one that includes popular sites like Metacrawler, Ask Jeeves and Dogpile. These sites—also called metasearch tools—don't maintain any kind of index of their own but instead issue search requests to fistfuls of other Web search sites. When Yahoo!, Hotbot, AltaVista and the like return their results, the metasearch site collects them onto a single Web page for display.

Because no two search sites index exactly the same set of Web pages, metasearch tools give you a wider scope of results—but it's worth remembering that more does not necessarily equal better. What really counts is relevant results that are sorted in a relevant order. And that's the rub.

Simply picking one of two or three types of sites to search from is no guarantee of good results.

Brad Hill, the author of *World Wide Web Searching for Dummies* (IDG), says most search sites deliver too much information. "Search engines do a good job on indexing," he said. But because of that, they deliver more than you want.

So when you're faced with several hundred thousand results over dozens of pages, what should you do? "Don't go past the first page of results," Hill said. "If it doesn't have something of interest, you've probably entered the wrong search string."

Most people could get much more relevant results with a few simple tricks for constructing a search "string"—the words you enter in the search box. The most obvious is to type in several relevant words instead of just one or two. In general, the fewer words you enter, the more general your results will be.

But not every search engine returns the most relevant results first—which leads to lots of pages about Lincoln Continentals instead of Lincoln's most famous speech. To give a search engine more instructions, it helps to master a site's instructions, which search techies call "operators."

"Search operators tell a search engine how to interpret your key words," Hill said. "Words like 'and' or 'not,' and quotation marks can really narrow down search results."

And it's narrowing the results—giving fewer, better pages—that really counts.

"The simplest techniques, like using quotes around a phrase, help the most people," Ms. Rex said. The result of slapping quotation marks around two or more words is remarkable. Type in "Gettysburg Address," with quotation marks, and you tell the search engine to look for a phrase instead of two separate words—knocking irrelevant vacation sites and real-estate listings out of your top 20 results.

That trick works in many search sites, including Yahoo!, AltaVista, Hotbot, Excite and Infoseek.

Not all search sites use the same rules for making better searches. Most will let you exclude some terms from your results—which is great if you're trying to search for, say, the gross national product of Jordan and keep getting sports sites about Michael Jordan. Exclude the word Michael, and you'll trim a few hundred thousand irrelevant results right away.

But how you exclude words from a search depends on the search site. In the regular search forms at Yahoo!, Excite and AltaVista, for example, you put a minus sign before the word (−Michael). But in Hotbot, you click on the More Search Options button and select Must Not Contain in the Word Filter section.

It is hardly surprising that many people find Web searching confusing and inefficient. So how are you supposed to know which rules apply to which search site? Karin Rex includes a simple piece of advice in lesson one of her Internet search class.

"Read the instructions," she said. "The only way to learn the inner workings of each site is to read the help files or frequently asked questions document. Most people don't even realize there are help files, so they'll never be able to take advantage of advanced features."

Sage advice though this is, search sites tend to use jargon that's not easily understood by the uninitiated. A single mention of Boolean operators is enough to send many would-be searchers into a tailspin. (Named for a 19th-century British mathematician, George Boole, Boolean operators are words like AND, OR and NOT that many advanced search sites use to make searches more precise.) But in truth, Boolean logic is not hard to learn—and in many cases, search sites label it with easy-to-understand phrasing like "search for ANY of these terms" or "search for these terms as a phrase."

There are options for sufferers of Boolean anxiety, though. One site with a novel approach is Ask Jeeves. When you enter a vague query, Ask Jeeves will throw back a series of questions. From the single-word query "travel," for example, it comes back with 10 possible interpretations of what you might be looking for, including "Where can I rent a cellular phone in a foreign country?" and "Where can I get tourist information about foreign countries?"

Another approach is to reduce the scope of your search. Searching the entire Web for a highly specialized piece of information isn't always the best way. For one thing, many Web search engines index only Web pages in HTML format, and many Web pages are generated from databases that search engine spiders can't penetrate. To uncover information from these databases, you usually need to use the search engine provided at the database's Web site. There are literally thousands of these highly specialized Web search tools across the Web.

So how can you find these specialized search tools? About 3,000 of them are listed at Internet Sleuth in Yahoo!-style directories. But unlike Yahoo!'s directories, Internet Sleuth's include only searchable sites and include the search form to issue a query right away.

No matter what advice you get, however, you discover the best search techniques by experimenting. Danny Sullivan of Search Engine Watch uses all the major search sites frequently, and refuses to name his favorite site. His reason?

"Judging the results is subjective," Sullivan said. "If your friend raves about a site and you don't like it, try another. Use whatever you find gives you the answers."

The New York Times, September 3, 1998
http://www.nytimes.com/library/tech/98/09/circuits/articles/03sear.html

CRITICAL THINKING QUESTIONS

1. Under what circumstances would you search the Web using a Web directory? Search site? Metasearch site?
2. Why does the same word or phrase yield different results with the various search sites?
3. What procedures would you suggest for improving your Web searches? Which of these procedures would work for all search engines? Which would be specific to the search engine?

SHORT APPLICATION ASSIGNMENTS

1. In teams of three to five, or as a class, discuss your responses to the preceding critical thinking questions.
2. Prepare a one-page memo report (200–250 words) to your instructor in which you respond to the critical thinking questions and offer a final summary of the article. You will find a model one-page report on the Web site (nytimes.swcollege.com).

3. Write an executive summary (200–250 words). As an administrative assistant to a busy executive, you are expected to summarize selected articles and present important points. You will find a model executive summary on the Web site.
4. Summarize this article (100–125 words) for your company's newsletter. You will find a model newsletter article on the Web site.
5. Using the same topic, search a Web directory and search site. Which results did you like best? Your instructor may ask you to share your results in a five-minute presentation or one-page memo.
6. Read, then practice using a search site's advanced features. Your instructor may ask you to share your results in a five-minute presentation or one-page memo.

BUILDING RESEARCH SKILLS

1. Individually or in teams, outline guidelines for searching the Web. Your instructor may ask you to submit a three to five page guide or post a Web page explaining Web search guidelines.
2. Using at least three other references (books, journal articles, newspaper stories, magazine stories or credible Web sites) write an 800- to 1,000-word essay addressing two of the preceding critical thinking questions. Assume that this essay is a background document for a corporation's research guidelines.
3. Using at least three other references (books, journal articles, newspaper stories, magazine stories or credible Web sites) post an 800- to 1,000-word Web page addressing at least two of the preceding critical thinking questions. Assume that this page is a background document for a corporation's research guidelines

Whales in the Minnesota River?
Only on the Web, Where Skepticism Is a Required Navigational Aid

By Tina Kelley

Tourists drove six hours to Mankato, Minn., in search of underground caves and hot springs mentioned on a Web site. When they arrived, there were no such attractions.

People searching for a discussion of Amnesty International's views on Tunisia learned about human rights in that North African country—but from supporters of the Tunisian authorities, not from the human rights group. The government supporters brought surfers to a site with a soothing Web address: www.amnesty-tunisia.org.

And bibliophiles who trust the grande dame of on-line retailers, Amazon.com, for suggestions under the headings of "Destined for Greatness" and "What We're Reading" were dismayed to learn that some publishers had paid for special treatment for their books—meaning a more accurate heading would have been "What We're Paid to Say We're Reading." (After the disclosure, Amazon added a note on its home page to make a subtle acknowledgement of the practice.)

On the World Wide Web, straight facts can be hard to find. After plowing through dense and recalcitrant search engines that offer more sites than you can point a mouse at, after enduring delays, lost links and dead ends and arriving at a site that looks just right, Web surfers must deal with uncertainty: Is the information true, unbiased and free of hidden sales pitches?

Even though it is easy to fall prey to parodies, politics, payola and ignorance on line, solid, watertight information can indeed be found on the Web.

But experts on Internet research point out that the Web is largely unregulated and unchecked, and so they agree that it is wise to be skeptical: Consider the source. Reconsider the source. Is the information up to date and professional and traceable? Can it be verified, or the source checked, off line? And just who was that source again?

Don Ray, a freelance investigative reporter in Burbank, Calif., and the author of *Checking Out Lawyers* (MIE Publishing, 1997), has what he calls a J.D.L.R. test to apply to Web research. "There should be a switch in every Internet user that toggles when something Just Doesn't Look Right," he said, "to make them re-evaluate the credibility of the source." If a Web page has grammatical errors, sloppy spelling or a goofy design, that makes him distrust the content.

And people who are getting ready to spend money on the basis of Web information should, of course, approach their decisions with at least as much skepticism as they would use about a purchase off line.

Whoppers have found a home on the Web since the very beginning. Yet for many people, computers have generally been treated as authority figures, able to calculate compound interest in a single bound. A machine that has been perfected by institutions of higher learning and is relied on by the Government isn't likely to lie, is it?

"We've inherited this notion that if it pops up on a screen and looks good, we tend to think of it as fairly credible," said Paul Gilster, author of *Digital Literacy* (Wiley Computer Publishing, 1997.)

Although the Web has come to resemble a monstrous library system where everyone has a printing press and all information is seemingly created equal, even the newest surfers come to it with useful information-sorting skills from the off-line world. They can differentiate among information from a trusted newspaper, a bulk mailing from a charity, a sales pitch from a stockbroker and a letter from a friend. They can distinguish commercial broadcasts from public television programs. They can skim over the pages in *Reader's Digest* with "Advertisement" printed at the top.

But on the Web, the clues for credibility are different, and so are the tools needed to assess the information.

How can someone know if a favorite portal site is making a nanobuck in sales commission every time the person buys something at the florist featured on the page? Comments from people who are either touting or trashing a stock on the Web for their own financial gain have been investigated repeatedly by the Federal Government. And is that medical information on that site underwritten by a drug company or by someone on drugs?

Research specialists agree on the importance of determining who finances a site and what profit motives may be at work. While the boundary between news material and advertising is fairly clearly marked in many print publications, on the Web the signals pointing to paid content are often subtle or nonexistent, or vary widely from site to site.

Amazon.com's practice is only the most visible of many arrangements between Internet companies—including one involving *The New York Times*.

The Web site of *The Times* includes, on book review pages, links to Barnes andnoble.com; *The Times* receives commissions from the resulting sales.

Of course, off-line retail stores—including bookstores and groceries—have long accepted pay for product placement. And being a knowledgeable consumer is important on line as well as off line.

At Time Warner's Pathfinder Network, Andrew Weil's theories on vitamins and health are used to create a profile of your vitamin needs and—surprise, surprise—sell you vitamins at the end (cgi.pathfinder.com/drweil/vitamin profiler).

Or consider www.smokefreekids.com, which presents all kinds of information on smoke-free dining and how to kick the nicotine habit—and won't let visitors miss out on the opportunity to buy No Smoke software to quit smoking.

Even outright spoofs can deceive the unwary Web traveler. Take the case of a site posted through Mankato State University by people fed up with the cold winters. The Mankato, Minn., Home Page advertised sunny beaches, an underwater city and whale watching on the Minnesota River (www.lme. mankato.msus.edu/mankato/mankato.html). Deep at the bottom of the disclaimer page one finds: "Mankato, as portrayed on these pages, DOES NOT EXIST! PLEASE do not come here to see these sites." Er, sights. (Of course, anybody looking at a map would probably be suspicious about the site's statement that "the winter temperature in many Mankato neighborhoods has never dropped below a balmy 70 degrees!")

That Mankato site "has caused some bad publicity for us," said Maureen Gustafson, head of the Mankato Area Chamber and Convention Bureau. "There was a guy who drove here from Canada with his son who was really ticked," she said. "And another one from Kansas."

She wrote the site's creator a letter—which he later posted, to her dismay—suggesting that he and his companions go play with Game Boys rather than undercut the city's promotional efforts.

Some Web sites appear designed to mislead or even intercept surfers, sometimes for political reasons. For instance, to counter what it calls intentionally misleading information, Amnesty International, the human rights group, has posted www.amnesty.org/tunisia, which includes point-by-point refutations of the site at www.amnesty-tunisia.org, which Amnesty calls "official Tunisian Internet propaganda." The Internet addresses of the pages are, of course, very close, adding to the confusion. But most surfers who wanted impartial information about Tunisia would perhaps choose not to rely on a site that prominently features a quotation from the president of Tunisia, Zine el-Abidine Ben Ali.

In a medium where truth is so elusive, medical misinformation is all too easy to find. Beth Mark, a librarian at Messiah College in Grantham, Pa., said a friend had sent her husband, Ken, an article from a commercial Web site (munkey.com/health/markle.html) about the health risks of the artificial sweetener aspartame. Mr. Mark, a diabetic, had recently suffered a mini-stroke, and he became worried after reading in the article that aspartame in the sodas he drinks could cause numbness, a claim that is generally not supported by scientific studies, although other questions have been raised about aspartame.

"It is sensational and contains unfounded claims regarding aspartame causing symptoms of M.S., numbness, etc.," Mrs. Mark said of the article, via e-mail.

Soon after, a senior medical adviser to the Multiple Sclerosis Foundation,

Dr. David Squillacote, posted a refutation of the article's claims (www.msfacts. org/aspartame.htm).

Deborah Cestone, head of the library and media department at the Pelham Memorial High School and Middle School in Pelham, N.Y., teaches students how to evaluate Web sources for their research papers.

"You'll find sites like the University of Pennsylvania Cancer Center, and you know that's good solid information, but then you'll find a paper done by some 10th grader as a project, and he's created a Web page from it," she said.

After all, anyone with an Internet service provider and a quarter to call it can set up a Web page that looks as official as a 1040 form, without the quality control that used to come from editors, fact checkers and large publishing houses. There are few barriers to bad information on line.

"If you wanted to publish a book that says 2 plus 2 equals 5, you had to go through a lot of effort and spend a great deal of money," said Tara Calishain, co-author of *The Official Netscape Guide to Internet Research* (International Thomson Publishing, 1998). "But the cost of putting up a Web page saying 2 plus 2 equals 5 is virtually nothing."

Genie Tyburski, a law librarian in Philadelphia, runs a site about reliable research on line (www.virtualchase.com), which includes pointers on how to avoid being duped. "Many of us who are my age, 41, grew up trusting print," she said. "If we read it, it must have been true. We translate that same comfort to the Web, where it's much more dangerous."

She recalled a Web site about the medical uses of marijuana that had been run from a man's personal home page. It included copies of articles from medical journals but no mention of permission to reproduce them, she said.

"With the technology of the Web, there's no barrier to editing," she said. "An entire interview reproduced in the article on the bogus site was not in the original article at all, and there were graphs to support certain statements that weren't in the original article."

Rob Rosenberger, a computer security expert, set up a Web site to dispel myths about computer viruses (www.kumite.com).

"I just claim to be unaligned, but how do you know that?" Mr. Rosenberger said in an interview. To encourage critical thinking, he has a link on his site titled "Learn About Rob Before You Start Taking His Advice," which dares people to treat his writing with the same skepticism he brings to virus scares.

Of course, it is hard to know who is paying whom for what kind of Internet presence. "There are the ones we know about, like Amazon.com, which got caught," Mr. Rosenberger said.

"But there are unscrupulous people in the securities industry who are trying to pump up or drive down stocks, to buy at low prices and sell at high prices, who may not be disclosing their fiduciary interests."

"People send out spams on the greatest I.P.O. on the Internet this year, or trash an I.P.O. that's going to occur, so they can get in at the low end," Mr. Rosenberger said. "We know that goes on, too."

Mr. Gilster, the author of *Digital Literacy*, said Internet users need to be trained to triangulate in on the truth.

"We need to set up content evaluation as part of the intellectual super-structure here and explain it to kids," he said, "so we end up with students who can use the Web intelligently and know when to cast grave doubt on a particular Web site. People have to be their own editors and take that upon themselves. Once you begin doing that, the habits become second nature."

But some questions about the validity of Web sources are impossible to answer beyond a reasonable doubt without stepping outside the hermetic box of the Internet. In such cases, no combination of pixels is sure to help.

"When you want to check citations, your librarian is your best friend," Ms. Calishain said. "There's a lot of stuff on line, but working with librarians is one of best things you can do with research. They're trained to classify information, and they can help you out."

It is also true that many librarians are learning to navigate the world of the Web, and they may just point an information-hungry consumer elsewhere.

Ms. Cestone, the Pelham school librarian, said she worked hard teaching students how to evaluate what might be the best resource for a given research problem.

"It may be the Internet is the best resource, or maybe a book, or maybe a person will be the best resource," she said.

The New York Times, March 4, 1999
http://www.nytimes.com/library/tech/99/03/circuits/articles/04trut.html

CRITICAL THINKING QUESTIONS

1. Is a Web site's information true, unbiased and free of hidden sales pitches?
2. How and why would organizations or individuals post Web sites containing misleading information?
3. What can be done to police misleading information on the Web?

SHORT APPLICATION ASSIGNMENTS

1. In teams of three to five, or as a class, discuss your responses to the preceding critical thinking questions.
2. Write an executive summary (200–250 words). As an administrative assistant to a busy executive, you are expected to summarize selected articles and present important points. You will find a model executive summary on the Web site (nytimes.swcollege.com).

3. Search the Web for information on a topic of your choice. Next, evaluate the credibility of the first three Web sites your chosen search engine returned. Which sites would you trust, and why? Your instructor may ask you to share your results in a five-minute presentation or one-page memo.

BUILDING RESEARCH SKILLS

1. Using at least three other references (books, journal articles, newspaper stories, magazine stories or credible Web sites) write an 800- to 1,000-word essay addressing two of the preceding critical thinking questions. Assume that this essay is a background document for a corporation's research guidelines.
2. Using at least three other references (books, journal articles, newspaper stories, magazine stories or credible Web sites) post an 800- to 1,000-word Web page addressing at least two of the preceding critical thinking questions. Assume that this page is a background document for a corporation's research guidelines.

CHAPTER 6

Communication to Persuade

PREVIEW

Business communication often persuades. The message may attempt to reject a customer's credit application while keeping the customer happy, ask a supplier for an additional discount or solicit sponsorship for a charity event.

Controversial at times, entertaining at times, the advertising industry continues to refine the art of persuasion. Actually, as William E. Geist shows in "Selling Soap to Children and Hairnets to Women," thanks to the pioneering work of Edward L. Bernays, persuasion is a science as well an art.

Still, there are multitudes of persuasion styles. In "Primers of Persuasion: How to Win With Words," Deborah Stead reviews four books about persuasion, ranging from contemporary titles like Gerry Spence's best-selling *How to Argue and Win Every Time* or Robert Mayer's *Power Plays: How to Negotiate, Persuade, and Finesse Your Way to Success in Any Situation*, to Dale Carnegie's 1937 classic, *How to Win Friends and Influence People*.

Lastly, Sabra Chartrand demonstrates how today's modern worker could persuade their employers to consider an alternative work style in "Building an Argument for Telecommuting."

Source: Christine M. Thompson/CyberTimes

Selling Soap to Children and Hairnets to Women

By William E. Geist

Edward Bernays originated the field of public relations about 60 years ago, and when he looks about him now and sees all that he has wrought, sometimes he thinks maybe he should have gone bowling instead.

The elfin 93-year-old was showing little remorse yesterday, however, accepting a plaque for his achievements from Dr. John Brademas, president of New York University—where in 1923 Mr. Bernays taught the first course anywhere in public relations—and basking in the applause of a lecture hall filled with the next generation of highly trained public relations people. "Image is the most important thing you have," said one of the students. "Face it."

Mr. Bernays, whose clients have included Presidents Coolidge, Wilson, Hoover and Eisenhower, as well as Edison, Freud, Caruso, Nijinsky, scores of the largest corporations and many foreign countries, told the students the story of his campaign to change the negative opinion children held toward soap by establishing an Ivory soap sculpture contest that soon had some 22 million children carving.

At one point early on in his career, after he had done some propaganda work for the Allies during World War I, it dawned on Mr. Bernays that, hey, he could mold public opinion. The dawning of public relations was at hand.

Press agents already existed—the famous Ivy Lee among them—but Mr. Bernays thought beyond press releases to trying actually to change the tides of public opinion—be it about bacon, bananas, Lithuania, a world war or Venida Hair Nets.

"Once," he said, nearly shuddering at the thought, "there was no public relations, and public opinion was at the mercy of the whimsical forces of chance. Businessmen were at the mercy of these same forces."

Mr. Bernays told the story of Irene Castle, dancer and idol, who got a bob haircut, and millions of women stormed the beauty parlors to copy the short style. "Hairnet makers were in a state of panic!" he recalled. "Hairpin manufacturers were laying off workers. The hair comb industry was in disarray."

Taking emergency action, Mr. Bernays arranged for safety experts to issue warnings of—precisely—what could happen if a woman went to work without a hairnet and got her hair caught in the machinery. Health experts came forward to speak of the horrors of food contamination if cooks and waitresses worked without hairnets. Laws were hastily passed in many states making hairnets mandatory.

For the American Tobacco Company, Mr. Bernays discovered that women were not smoking Lucky Strikes because the green packages clashed with almost every color of women's garments. But the president of American Tobacco refused to change the package, and so Mr. Bernays set about trying to make green the predominant color of women's fashion. By several accounts, he succeeded, after holding a "Green Ball" for the most famous of socialites, after having green garments featured in *Vogue* and *Harpers Bazaar*, and then convincing manufacturers to make green the new color. "All things are possible in New York," he said, "which was and is the center of communications."

Women bought more cigarettes, just as they did after he made smoking cigarettes in public a feminist issue. Long before "You've Come A Long Way Baby," Mr. Bernays arranged for the debutantes in several cities to gather in public places at a set hour to light up their Luckies—also known as Torches of Freedom.

When research linking cigarette smoking to cancer was revealed, he turned around and worked to have cigarette commercials banned from television. "That's the P.R. game," he said with a shrug.

His modus operandi from the start was obtaining endorsements from "opinion leaders" as well as favorable results from experiments and surveys conducted by doctors and panels of experts. His in-depth research and applied psychology was all rather startling in the early days as he was criticized for manipulating public opinion. It was called "the new science of ballyhoo."

What was the poor unorganized and helpless consumer, the poor voter, to do as the torrential, sophisticated propaganda came raining down upon him?

Mr. Bernays is a nephew of Freud—Mr. Bernays has 52 letters from him— and there are those who contend that Mr. Bernays has had nearly as much influence on life in this century as his famous uncle.

Sharp as a tack at 93, Mr. Bernays still does some work for clients.

He allows as how he may have created something of a monster with this public relations. "Everyone has a press agent now," he said, "or a media consultant or communications director or whatever you want to call it. Some of Nixon's people who went to jail called themselves public relations people. Image has become everything. Look what's happened in politics."

"Sometimes," he said, "it seems sort of like discovering a medicine to cure a disease, and then finding out that so much of it is being administered that people are getting sick from the overdoses."

The New York Times, March 27, 1985
http://www.nytimes.com/books/98/08/16/specials/bernays-selling.html

CRITICAL THINKING QUESTIONS

1. Can public relations and similar persuasion techniques mold others' opinions? Why, or why not?
2. What role does research play in the persuasion process?

3. In public relations, "image is everything," said Mr. Bernays. Is this true? Why, or why not?
4. When, if ever, is persuasion unethical?
5. What persuasive techniques work in business communication?

SHORT APPLICATION ASSIGNMENTS

1. In teams of three to five, or as a class, discuss your responses to the preceding critical thinking questions.
2. Prepare a one-page memo report (200–250 words) to your instructor in which you respond to the critical thinking questions and offer a final summary of the article. You will find a model one-page report on the Web site (nytimes.swcollege.com).
3. Write an executive summary (200–250 words). As an administrative assistant to a busy executive, you are expected to summarize selected articles and present important points. You will find a model executive summary on the Web site.
4. Summarize this article (100–125 words) for your company's newsletter. You will find a model newsletter article on the Web site.
5. In teams of three to five, or as a class, review the press releases on a school's Web site. Are the press releases trying to persuade you? What persuasive techniques have the press releases used. Your instructor may assign you an organization and ask you to share your results in a five-minute presentation or one-page memo.
6. In teams of three to five, or as a class, create a campaign that persuades children to eat more broccoli. Your instructor may ask you to share your results in a five-minute presentation or one-page memo.

BUILDING RESEARCH SKILLS

1. Individually or in teams, create a campaign that persuades children to eat more broccoli. Your instructor may ask you to submit a three- to five-page policy handbook or post a Web page, along with a letter of transmittal explaining the project.
2. Using at least three other references (books, journal articles, newspaper stories, magazine stories or credible Web sites) write an 800- to 1,000-word essay addressing two of the preceding critical thinking questions.
3. Using at least three other references (books, journal articles, newspaper stories, magazine stories or credible Web sites) post an 800- to 1,000-word Web page addressing at least two of the preceding critical thinking questions.

Primers of Persuasion:
How to Win With Words

By Deborah Stead

A friend of mine, a lawyer doing business in the former Soviet sphere, once told me about a contract he negotiated for some American businessmen investing in a Russian enterprise during the old perestroika days.

His clients wanted to be able to sue their Soviet partner, despite its state-owned status, if the deal soured. So they asked for a waiver of sovereign immunity claims. The Russians, who like parity in their pacts, said they'd agree only if the American company signed the same waiver. "But we're private, not an arm of a nation; we don't have any sovereign immunity to begin with," the lawyer explained. Then, contemplating the stony stares on the other side of the table and realizing he had nothing to lose, he affably "gave in" to the demand.

That's the difference between people who have a knack for negotiating and those of us who can't win a round with the wedding caterer, let alone the comrades. (When I was a mother of the bride, an "M.O.B.," as the catering contract called me, my performance at the negotiating table forced me to cede all bargaining power to the B., who deemed my method—repeating the same request 15 different ways and occasionally muttering "That's not fair"—exasperating and odd.)

So what is the art of the deal? As described in some recent books on bargaining, it's martial. It's mental judo, where you use the other guy's energy to win. It's mind-set. It's charisma.

That's the message of *Power Plays: How to Negotiate, Persuade, and Finesse Your Way to Success in Any Situation*, by Robert Mayer (Times Business Books, $25). Mr. Mayer preaches what he presumably practices at Mayer, Glassman & Gaines, his Los Angeles law firm: the gospel of Lancer.

"Lancer," its combative ring aside, stands for a string of nonviolent nouns: linkage, alignment, needs, control, evaluation and reading. The idea is to use these principles to get on the path of no resistance.

The motto for this could be: Don't muscle, manipulate. You link and align, for example, by using the other person's words and stifling the urge to use confrontational phrases. "If saying it will make you feel good," the author advises, "then don't say it unless it will make the other person feel good." (And this guy has divorce clients?)

Next, listen for the unspoken demands. What psychological needs drive your counterpart? Self-esteem? The quest to belong? Find out, the author says, because a hidden agenda can be key to the negotiation. Try to control the proceedings subtly, with questions, judicious interruptions and the channeling of information, sandwiching the weak part of your presentation between two stronger items, for example.

And try to read other people by noting how they position themselves: Sitting at an angle from you signals unease. Sitting directly across indicates confidence or that they've read this book.

The E, if you're keeping track, is for evaluation, but somehow this has to do with the power connotations of faxing, e-mailing or taking phone calls. Why evaluation? I figure the author needed a vowel for his mnemonic word. (How about "exchange?")

So much for the theory behind Mr. Mayer's nonthreatening approach, which in many ways builds on the principles laid out long ago in Dale Carnegie's *How to Win Friends and Influence People,* still an international best seller and first published by Simon & Schuster in 1937. (Those Russian entrepreneurs should have picked up a copy. A Russian version is a big seller in Moscow metro stations.) If you're curious about this primer of persuasion, look for the Pocket Book paperback ($5.99).

Getting to Yes: Negotiating Agreement Without Giving In, by Roger Fisher and William Ury (Penguin, $11.95), published by Houghton Mifflin in 1981, is another negotiating guide in this soft mode, although it reaches further than most how-to books by taking up issues of politics and diplomacy

Gerry Spence's book, the best selling *How to Argue and Win Every Time* (St. Martin's Press, $22.95), also carries a love-thy-adversary tone. The book, which will be out in paperback this spring, contends that the art of argument is the art of living—an interesting thought, and no doubt true for top-notch litigators like Mr. Spence. The author, a self-described country lawyer, occasionally lathers on the down-home stuff—you'd think you were reading "Getting to Yup"—and the prose can get awfully purple. But maybe those are the right touches for inspirational books like this one. For me, the tales from the courtroom worked best.

Mr. Mayer's "Power Play" also is best when it goes beyond the I'm-no-threat tradition. What to do if the kindler, gentler stuff fails? It's time to bargain hard, the author says, describing intriguing ways to break a deadlock or come up with hard figures acceptable to both sides. Many lawyers probably know about some of these solutions, games he calls "golf" and "baseball," but lay people may find some fresh ideas here.

The author really finds his voice in the section he calls the "Playbook," a list of "tips, tricks and tactics" for negotiating discounts on appliances (have the sales clerk invest time in you), surviving an I.R.S. audit and—as they say in that hard-sell school of persuasion—much, much more.

The New York Times, March 3, 1996
http://www.nytimes.com/books/business/9603shelf.html

CRITICAL THINKING QUESTIONS

1. Is successful negotiation a case of your side, or both sides, winning? Why?
2. How would negotiating principles apply to business communication?
3. Is all business communication a form of negotiation? Why, or why not?
4. Should one take a soft or hard approach to negotiating? Why?

SHORT APPLICATION ASSIGNMENTS

1. In teams of three to five, or as a class, discuss your responses to the preceding critical thinking questions.
2. Prepare a one-page memo report (200–250 words) to your instructor in which you respond to the critical thinking questions and offer a final summary of the article. You will find a model one-page report on the Web site (nytimes.swcollege.com).
3. Write an executive summary (200–250 words). As an administrative assistant to a busy executive, you are expected to summarize selected articles and present important points. You will find a model executive summary on the Web site.
4. Summarize this article (100–125 words) for your company's newsletter. You will find a model newsletter article on the Web site.
5. Should business communication be a required course? In two teams of three to five each, take opposite sides of the issue. Negotiate an answer to the question. Your instructor may ask you to share your results in a five-minute presentation or one-page memo.

BUILDING RESEARCH SKILLS

1. Read one of the books mentioned in the story. How does the book's information relate to business communication? Your instructor may ask you to submit a three to five-page report or post a Web page explaining the business communication information you found.
2. Using at least three other references (books, journal articles, newspaper stories, magazine stories or credible Web sites) write an 800- to 1,000-word essay addressing two of the preceding critical thinking questions. Assume that this essay will be used as an internal reference for a corporation's Internet manual.
3. Using at least three other references (books, journal articles, newspaper stories, magazine stories or credible Web sites) post an 800- to 1,000-word Web page addressing at least two of the preceding critical thinking questions. Assume that this page will be posted on a corporate intranet.

Building an Argument for Telecommuting

By Sabra Chartrand

If you get the job done, does it matter whether your boss actually sees you doing it?

For many workers, the answer is "absolutely!,"—the tree falling in the forest makes no sound if no one is there to see it. Even if the job isn't getting done, many people still want their boss to notice them sitting at their desk or putting in overtime on a weekend. Simply being on the job can earn points for commitment, loyalty, team-work. There's even a name for those idle hours spent at work just to show a presence—"face time."

But the need to be seen toiling away (or appearing to toil) cannot co-exist with the growing interest many workers have in flexible scheduling, telecommuting and other family-friendly policies. They want to be able to tend to their children or aging parents without feeling like their colleagues consider them to be shirking their job responsibilities.

Already, many companies have enacted flexibility policies as a way to help their employees balance personal and work lives. Every month many others begin to consider such alternative working arrangements, or start testing their practice. But even at those companies, many people are still reluctant to take advantage of the opportunity to work from home occasionally. Fear stymies requests for the flexibility to telecommute—fear that the boss and colleagues will assume anyone who wants to telecommute isn't committed to their job, that work is not the most important part of their life.

At companies where no one has yet breached the wall that keeps flexibility out, the fear of sending the wrong signal can be even greater. But there are strategies for convincing a manager or corporate employer to experiment with flexibility and other family-friendly benefits.

Computer communications software, modems and laptops, the Internet, e-mail and fax machines, and cellular phones have eased working from home, a hotel or a customer's office. Telecommuting is as common in Silicon Valley as having a desk in the company headquarters. But it is virtually unheard of on Wall Street. In between, nearly half of American businesses allow workers some kind of flexible scheduling.

If telecommuting once or twice a week is appealing, prepare a strategy for convincing your supervisor or employer that it is in his interest, too. Don't raise the idea while feeling like you're asking for permission to stay home and goof off.

Approach the suggestion as you would any business proposal. There has to be more to it than just the desire to be home when the kids get out of school. Research the options, document the advantages, and present your boss with a well-laid strategy. Be able to explain to your boss how telecommuting will help both of you—how you'll get your job done, remain committed to the company and save it money, too.

In other words, answer his questions before he can raise them:

- How will this affect your productivity?
- How will it affect your relationship with your colleagues and supervisors?
- How will you brainstorm with co-workers or put together a team to pursue a client, design a new product or compile a report?
- How will you get support and feedback?
- What part of your job can you do easily, or better, at home?
- What part must be left for your days in the office?
- How will the company's goals remain a priority and still be met?
- How will you create a workplace in your home?
- How will you deliver materials back and forth to the office?
- How will customers or clients interact with you?

Many of the answers will be unique to your position—so analyze your job responsibilities, your typical workday, your goals for yourself and your company's expectations as you prepare your proposal.

Other answers can be applied to many professionals who want to telecommute. For instance, flexible scheduling and other family-oriented policies can save companies money because they cut absenteeism and boost employee retention. In addition, research has demonstrated that telecommuters are frequently 10 to 20 percent more productive than office and other traditional workplace workers. Productivity can increase because there are fewer distractions during work hours, and less time wasted on commuting.

More important, productivity can increase once a worker makes his job project-oriented instead of time-oriented. He can argue to his boss that if he meets his goals and deadlines efficiently and successfully, it shouldn't matter how much time it took to complete the task or when he put in the hours. His commitment to his job can be judged on his performance, not on how many minutes he spent at his desk.

Answers to these and other questions are not difficult to find at telecommuting-related sites all over the Internet. Already, nearly eight million workers telecommute to their jobs. That leaves many millions more to raise the idea with their bosses.

CyberTimes, The New York Times on the Web, July 6, 1997
http://www.nytimes.com/library/jobmarket/070697sabra.html

CRITICAL THINKING QUESTIONS

1. How would telecommuting affect business communication?

2. If you get the job done, does it matter whether your boss actually sees you doing it? Why, or why not?
3. Under what circumstances would telecommuting make sense? Not make sense?
4. What business communication tasks make sense for telecommuters? Why?
5. What questions should you address to determine if telecommuting makes sense for you?

SHORT APPLICATION ASSIGNMENTS

1. In teams of three to five, or as a class, discuss your responses to the preceding critical thinking questions.
2. Prepare a one-page memo report (200–250 words) to your instructor in which you respond to the critical thinking questions and offer a final summary of the article. You will fine a model one-page report on the Web site (nytimes.swcollege.com).
3. Write an executive summary (200–250 words). As an administrative assistant to a busy executive, you are expected to summarize selected articles and present important points. You will find a model executive summary on the Web site.
4. Summarize this article (100–125 words) for your company's newsletter. You will find a model newsletter article on the Web site.
5. In teams of three to five, or as a class, build a persuasive argument for telecommuting. Your instructor may give you a sample job, as well as ask you to share your results in a five-minute presentation or one-page memo.

BUILDING RESEARCH SKILLS

1. Individually or in teams, draft a telecommunication policy for an organization. Your instructor may give you a sample organization as well as ask you to submit a three- to five-page policy plan or post a Web page, along with a letter of transmittal explaining the project.
2. Using at least three other references (books, journal articles, newspaper stories, magazine stories or credible Web sites) write an 800- to 1,000-word essay addressing two of the preceding critical thinking questions. Assume that this essay is a background document for a corporation's marketing plan.
3. Using at least three other references (books, journal articles, newspaper stories, magazine stories or credible Web sites) post an 800- to 1,000-word Web page addressing at least two of the preceding critical thinking questions. Assume that this page is a background document for a corporation's marketing plan.

CHAPTER 7

Career Communication

PREVIEW

While plenty of business communication technologies exist, there is no guarantee that these technologies actually improve business communication. Technology does, however, open up new opportunities, such as searching for employment. At the same time, there are job-searching guidelines that have stood the test of time.

PowerPoint is one of the most popular presentation software packages today, but does PowerPoint improve a presentation? That depends, says Laurence Zuckerman in "Words Go Right to the Brain, but Can They Stir the Heart?" His story discusses how technology can help, or hurt, a presentation.

Technology, especially the Internet, has changed the way students seek employment. Two of many Internet examples are career Web sites and electronic résumés. Lisa Guernsey's "Students Search Web for First Real-World Jobs," explores the digital nuances of job-searching today.

Although technology helps, it by no means guarantees finding a job. Andrew Ross Sorkin explains the basic steps leading up to an interview as well as hints for the interview in "College and Money: And Never Lie About Your Grades."

Source: Christine M. Thompson/CyberTimes

Words Go Right to the Brain, but Can They Stir the Heart?

Some Say Popular Software Debases Public Speaking

By Laurence Zuckerman

Good Morning. The title of today's presentation is: "The Effect of Presentation Software on Rhetorical Thinking," or "Is Microsoft Powerpoint Taking Over Our Minds?"

I will begin by making a joke.

Then I will take you through each of my points in a linear fashion.

Then I will sum up again at the end. Unfortunately, because of the unique format of this particular presentation, we will not be able to entertain questions.

Were Willy Loman to shuffle through his doorway today instead of in the late 1940's, when Arthur Miller wrote "Death of a Salesman," he might still be carrying his sample case, but he would also be lugging a laptop computer featuring dozens of slides illustrating his strongest pitches complete with bulleted points and richly colored bars and graphs.

Progress? Many people believe that the ubiquity of prepackaged computer software that helps users prepare such presentations has not only taken much of the life out of public speaking by homogenizing it at a low level, but has also led to a kind of ersatz thought that is devoid of original ideas.

Scott McNealy, the shoot-from-the-lip chairman and chief executive of Sun Microsystems, who regularly works himself into a lather criticizing the Microsoft Corporation, announced two years ago that he was forbidding Sun's 25,000 employees to use Powerpoint, the Microsoft presentation program that leads the market. (The ban was not enforced.) Some computer conferences have expressly barred presenters from using slides as visual aids during their talks, because they think it puts too much emphasis on the sales pitch at the expense of content.

Psychologists, computer scientists and software developers are more divided about the effect of Powerpoint and its competitors. Some are sympathetic to the argument that the programs have debased public speaking to the level of an elementary school filmstrip.

"The tools we use to shape our thinking with the help of digital computers are not value free," said Steven Johnson, the author of *Interface Culture*, a 1997 study of the designs used to enable people to interact with computers.

Johnson uses Powerpoint himself (for example, during a recent talk he gave at Microsoft) but nonetheless said, "There is certain kind of Powerpoint logic that is brain numbing."

Presentation programs are primarily used for corporate and sales pitches. Still, the approach has leaked into the public discourse. Think of Ross Perot's graphs or President Clinton's maps. Critics argue such programs contribute to the debasement of rhetoric. "Try to imagine the 'I have a dream' speech with Powerpoint," said Cliff Nass, an associate professor of communication at Stanford University who specializes in human-computer interaction.

Other people, however, have made the opposite argument, saying that Powerpoint has elevated the general level of discourse by forcing otherwise befuddled speakers to organize their thoughts and by giving audiences a visual source of information that is a much more efficient way for humans to learn than by simply listening.

"We are visual creatures," said Steven Pinker, a psychology professor at the Massachusetts Institute of Technology and the author of several books about cognition including *The Language Instinct*. "Visual things stay put, whereas sounds fade. If you zone out for 30 seconds—and who doesn't?—it is nice to be able to glance up on the screen and see what you missed."

Pinker argues that human minds have a structure that is not easily reprogrammed by media. "If anything, Powerpoint, if used well, would ideally reflect the way we think," he said.

But Powerpoint too often is not used well, as even Pinker admitted. He is on a committee at M.I.T. that is updating the traditional writing requirement to include both speech and graphic communication. "M.I.T. has a reputation for turning out Dilberts," he said. "They may be brilliant in what they do, but no one can understand what they say."

Visual presentations have played an important part in business and academia for decades, if not centuries. One of the most primitive presentation technologies, the chalkboard, is still widely used. But in recent years the spread of portable computers has greatly increased the popularity of presentation programs.

Just as the word processing programs eliminated many of the headaches of writing on a typewriter, presentation software makes it easy for speakers to create slides featuring text or graphics to accompany their talks. The programs replace the use of overhead projectors and acetate transparencies, which take time to create and are more difficult to revise. Most lecture halls and conference rooms now feature screens that connect directly to portable computers, so speakers can easily project their visual aids.

The secret to Powerpoint's success is that it comes free with Microsoft's best-selling Office software package, which also features a word processing program and an electronic spreadsheet. Other presentation programs, like Freelance from I.B.M.'s Lotus division and Corel Corporation's Presentations, also come bundled with other software, but Office is by far the most successful, racking up $5.6 billion in sales last year.

Because most people do not buy Powerpoint on its own, it is difficult to tell how many actual users there are. Microsoft says that its surveys show that, compared with two years ago, twice as many people who have Office are regular users of Powerpoint today, and that three times as many Office users have at least tried the program. Anecdotal evidence indicates an explosion in the use of Powerpoint.

For instance, the program is used for countless sales pitches every day both inside and outside a wide variety of companies. It is de rigueur for today's M.B.A. candidates.

The Dale Carnegie Institute, which imbues its students with the philosophy of the man who wrote the seminal work *How to Win Friends and Influence People*, has a partnership with Microsoft and offers a course in "high-impact presentations" at its 170 training centers in 70 countries. Microsoft has incorporated into Powerpoint many templates based on the Carnegie programs and has even incorporated the Carnegie course into the program's help feature.

Powerpoint is so popular that in many offices it has entered the lexicon as a synonym for a presentation, as in "Did you send me the Powerpoint?"

The backlash against the program is understandable. Even before the advent of the personal computer, there were those who argued that speeches with visual aids stressed form over content. Executives at International Business Machines Corporation, the model of a successful corporation in the 1950's, 60's and 70's, were famous for their use of "foils," or transparencies.

"People learned that the way to get ahead wasn't necessarily to have good ideas," wrote Paul Carroll in "Big Blues," his 1993 study of I.B.M.'s dramatic decline in the era of the personal computer. "That took too long to become apparent. The best way to get ahead was to make good presentations."

Critics make many of the same claims about Powerpoint today. "It gives you a persuasive sheen of authenticity that can cover a complete lack of honesty," said John Gage, the chief scientist at Sun Microsystems, who is widely respected in the computer industry as a visionary.

Academic critics echo the arguments made by Max Weber and Marshall McLuhan ("The medium is the message") that form has a critical impact on content.

"Think of it as trying to be creative on a standardized form," Nass said. "Any technology that organizes and standardizes tends to homogenize."

Powerpoint may homogenize more than most. In the early 1990's Microsoft realized that many of its customers were not using Powerpoint for a very powerful reason: They were afraid. Steven Sinofsky, the Microsoft vice president in charge of the Office suite, said that writer's block was an issue for people using word processors and other programs but the problem was worse with Powerpoint because of the great fear people had of public speaking.

"What would happen was that people would start up Powerpoint and just stare at it," he said.

Microsoft's answer was the "autocontent wizard," an automated feature that guides users through a prepared presentation format based on what they are trying to communicate. There are templates for "Recommending a Strategy," "Selling a Product," "Reporting Progress" and "Communicating Bad News."

Since 1994, when it was first introduced, the autocontent wizard in Powerpoint has become increasingly sophisticated. About 15 percent of users, Sinofsky said, now start their presentations with one of those templates.

The latest version of Powerpoint, which will be released this month, will feature an even more powerful wizard. The new version also includes thousands of pieces of clip art that the program can suggest to illustrate slides. There is even a built-in presentation checker that will tell you whether your slides are too wordy, or that your titles should be capitalized while bullet points should be lower case.

Many see the best antidote to the spread of Powerpoint in a graphic medium that is expanding even faster than the use of presentation software: the Web. Whereas Powerpoint presentations are static and linear, the Web jumps around, linking information in millions of ways. Gage of Sun tries to use the Web to illustrate his many public speeches, though a live Internet connection is not as readily available at lecterns these days as a cable that can connect a notebook computer to a screen for a Powerpoint presentation.

"Powerpoint is just a step along the way because you can't click on a Powerpoint presentation and get the details," said Daniel S. Bricklin, who developed the first electronic spreadsheet for PC's and more recently a program called Trellix that puts Web-like links into documents.

Bricklin said the Web, like any new medium, required new forms of composition just as the headlines and opening paragraphs of newspaper articles helped readers skim for the most information.

But he does not bemoan the popularity of presentation software. "It was a lot worse," he said, "when people got up with their hands in their pockets, twirling their keys, going, 'Um um um.'"

The New York Times, April 17, 1999
http://www.nytimes.com/library/tech/99/04/biztech/articles/17power.html

CRITICAL THINKING QUESTIONS

1. Does popular presentation software debase public speaking? Why, or why not?
2. Does popular presentation software elevate the general level of discourse? Why, or why not?
3. When, if at all, is popular software appropriate for presentations?
4. How should one use popular software to improve a presentation?

SHORT APPLICATION ASSIGNMENTS

1. In teams of three to five, or as a class, discuss your responses to the preceding critical thinking questions.
2. Prepare a one-page memo report (200–250 words) to your instructor in which you respond to the critical thinking questions and offer a final summary of the article. You will find a model one-page report on the Web site (nytimes.swcollege.com).
3. Write an executive summary (200–250 words). As an administrative assistant to a busy executive, you are expected to summarize selected articles and present important points. You will find a model executive summary on the Web site.
4. Summarize this article (100–125 words) for your company's newsletter. You will find a model newsletter article on the Web site.
5. In teams of three to five, prepare two versions of the same presentation—with and without presentation software. Your instructor may ask you to give two five-minute presentations.

BUILDING RESEARCH SKILLS

1. Prepare two versions of the same presentation—with and without presentation software. Your instructor may ask you to give two fifteen-minute presentations.
2. Individually or in teams, summarize a policy for using presentation software. Your instructor may give you a sample company as well as ask you to submit a three to five page guide or post a Web page explaining attachment guidelines.
3. Using at least three other references (books, journal articles, newspaper stories, magazine stories or credible Web sites) write an 800- to 1,000-word essay addressing two of the preceding critical thinking questions.
4. Using at least three other references (books, journal articles, newspaper stories, magazine stories or credible Web sites) post an 800- to 1,000-word Web page addressing at least two of the preceding critical thinking questions.

Students Search Web for First Real-World Jobs

By Lisa Guernsey

It was 3 o'clock on a Wednesday morning, and Carla Arellano was sitting in front of her computer in her off-campus apartment, trying to keep her eyes open. In just a few hours, her résumé was due at Georgetown University's career center.

At that late hour, her main concern was making sure that her résumé had the right keywords. "I was trying to put certain words at the beginning of a sentence, so that a computer might catch it more easily," Ms. Arellano said, recalling that sleepless night. "'Analytical'—that was one of my words. And 'qualitative skills.' And 'consulting.'"

Ms. Arellano, a senior at Georgetown, was having her first encounter with a high-tech job search. She was building an electronic résumé that could easily be found once planted into a prospective employer's computerized database. She was also scouring the Internet for Web sites with résumé-writing advice and bookmarking job boards. But she wasn't finding the experience to be everything she expected.

"Everyone said that the Internet would help," she said, "but it was not as easy as everyone said it would be."

Before the Internet, job searches were done in person. College career offices were nerve centers on campus, as places where students would leaf through binders full of career information and sign up for interviews with employers who came to campus. Job fairs required attendance. The firm handshake and clear gaze were the order of the day.

Now most students visit career centers online first. They post résumés and search for job information on the Internet.

They may close the deal in person, but they often start in front of the computer.

New York University, for example, has developed an in-house system called Careernet that gives students online access to job postings aimed at N.Y.U. students. Georgetown has developed a Web-based scheduling system, through which students find out if they have been selected for interviews with employers coming to campus and then sign up for time slots. Columbia University uses a similar system that requires students to send their résumés to the career center electronically.

Most students in the job market are intimately familiar with their campus's career center Web site, even if they have never visited the office in person.

Kristi Syrdahl, an N.Y.U. junior, said she had had more luck with her university's Careernet than with nationwide job boards. She spent her winter break using her home computer to search for a summer job or internship. She found not one but two. She also found her current part-time job through the Careernet.

But many students feel the same ambivalence about electronic job hunting that Ms. Arellano did.

They love the Internet's speed and its breadth of information. Some students said they checked online job postings whenever they found themselves near a computer. But many of the same students are not hopeful about finding a job online. And they are wary about technology—instead of humans—making decisions about which jobs they might be qualified for.

This should be a good year to experiment with ways to find jobs, since there seem to be quite a few jobs out there. Employers who participated in a survey last fall by the National Association of Colleges and Employers forecasted a 10 percent increase in the number of openings this year. While the job market is not as flush as it was for 1998 graduates—who benefited from the best year this decade for job seekers—it is still quite strong, said Camille Luckenbaugh, the association's employment information manager.

As might be expected, jobs in information technology are some of the easiest to find, and as with many other high-tech positions, most of them are posted online. Some companies have devoted sections of their Web sites to recruitment, announcing job openings and requesting résumés. National online job boards like Monster.com and Careerpath list thousands of openings every day—many of which are in telecommunications, software and technical consulting industries. Job seekers can simply skim the job postings, or they may post digital versions of their résumés and fill out online forms that are compiled in databases viewed by employers.

Jobs for college grads without computer-science backgrounds, however, are harder to find using online job boards.

Monster.com has a "campus zone" and Career Mosaic has a "college connection" section. Both offer advice, but most of their listings are not aimed at people fresh out of college.

"Online searching wasn't very helpful," said Tony Oliver, an English major at Georgetown who was looking for a consulting job. "On Monster.com, I would get four to five e-mail messages a day, but they were geared to people with a lot of programming experience."

Patricia Esianor, a graduate student in public administration at New York University, said she had "been searching basically everything" but had not had much success online either. She posted her résumé on the Job Direct Web site.

"So far the feedback I've received has been for things I don't want to do, in places I don't want to go," she said. She wondered if a real human being was even reading her résumé.

"It seems as if a computer is reading it," she said. "It's too impersonal."

Despite such setbacks, most students still seem to visit online job boards

CONSUMER INFORMATION

Career counselors for college students offer this advice:
- List your computer skills on your résumé, even if you are not looking for a high-tech job.
- Don't include your Internet home page address on your résumé unless you have groomed the site for a business audience.
- Include your e-mail address, and check for messages often.
- Don't expect companies to open your e-mail attachments. Always send another copy of your résumé and cover letter as a text message in a fax or via postal mail.
- Before going to an interview, visit the employer's Web site. Know what's on it.
- For the most part, getting your foot in the door still entails getting your foot in the door. Try to line up in-person interviews when you can.

when starting their search. They are also putting a lot of energy into creating the perfect electronic résumé, sometimes called a "scannable" résumé, one without any special formatting or graphics that might trip up an optical scanner.

These days, most electronic résumés never even make it into print.

They are simply sent via e-mail or pasted into online forms. College career centers devote entire workshops to electronic résumés, teaching students how to send them as e-mail attachments or create text-only versions without tabs or line breaks that get garbled in transmission.

A few companies simply print out these résumés once they have arrived electronically. But some large corporations like Hewlett-Packard and Kaiser-Permanente feed them into résumé management data bases. Many of the data bases organize the résumés by matching words in them with a list of keywords that the companies are looking for. Seeding a résumé with the right keywords can become a full-time obsession for some college seniors—particularly those business or computer science majors who hope to work for large companies.

George Tarnopolsky, a business management and marketing major at Cornell University, said he had even seen students add a section called "keywords" at the bottom of their résumés, right under "experience" and "education." Once the section is added, Tarnopolsky said, the number of times employers look at your résumé increases from "something like three times a week to five times a day." (People using Monster.com, for example, can check how many employers have looked at their résumés.)

Liberal arts students do not usually spend as much time focusing on key-words because their target employers are less likely to have large, automated résumé-management systems. And in general, these students may find the Web less useful. Many liberal arts students search for jobs in the nonprofit arena or at government agencies—positions that are often the hardest to find. Those employers do not often rely as heavily on national online job boards, like Careerpath. Also, nonprofit employers rarely have the resources to visit campuses for interviews.

Instead, such employers are starting to send job listings to college career centers, for posting on their online job boards. Or they send information about the positions to an online service called Jobtrak. Jobtrak maintains a data base of job openings for use by college career centers only. Employers send their job postings to Jobtrak and designate the colleges they would like to target. They pay $18 per listing per college, or less if they are posting to more than one. More than 800 campuses use the service.

To give employers yet another way to narrow their recruiting, the Ivy League schools, along with Stanford University and the Massachusetts Institute of Technology, served as hosts of an "Ivy+ Virtual Career Fair" two weeks ago. The one-week "fair" took place on the Web. Only students from the 10 elite colleges could enter. Once they logged in, they were required to add their résumés to an electronic book, which was open to employers. Students could browse job openings and ask employers questions via e-mail or online bulletin boards.

The Center for Arts and Culture, in Washington, was one of the 150 partici-pating employers. Malissa R. Bennett, programs and operations manager for the center, said that the fair was the center's first chance to actively recruit students online. She added that she was impressed with what she saw.

Still, she was not ready to go completely digital. When it came to accepting résumés, "I specifically asked for a paper submission," Ms. Bennett said. "Some applicants, those who seemed more serious about the job, took the time to send in a complete paper application with cover letter, résumé and writing sample."

An awareness of that perception hounds today's college grads. "E-mailing my résumé didn't get the same results as going to the career center and meet-ing companies," said Ms. Arellano, the Georgetown senior. "It seemed that e-mail wasn't taken as seriously by employers."

Ms. Arellano did get a job she wanted, as an information-technology analyst for Chase Manhattan Bank. But she landed it by meeting her employers face-to-face at an old-fashioned campus interview, with a paper résumé in hand.

She had mixed feelings looking back at those frenzied weeks she spent online.

Although she was able to do more research on the Web than would have been possible otherwise, she didn't like the impersonal nature of applying for jobs over a computer.

But she couldn't be happier about one use of the technology: When Chase decided to let her know that she would soon get a formal job offer, the bank sent her a quick note via e-mail.

The New York Times, April 28, 1999
http://www.nytimes.com/library/tech/99/04/circuits/articles/29jobs.html

CRITICAL THINKING QUESTIONS

1. How has the Internet changed job-hunting?
2. How should you electronically search, and apply, for jobs.
3. How do most companies analyze electronic résumés?
4. How, if at all, should electronic résumés differ from print résumés?
5. What are the advantages, and disadvantages, of searching for a job electronically?

SHORT APPLICATION ASSIGNMENTS

1. In teams of three to five, or as a class, discuss your responses to the preceding critical thinking questions.
2. Prepare a one-page memo report (200–250 words) to your instructor in which you respond to the critical thinking questions and offer a final summary of the article. You will find a model one-page report on the Web site (nytimes.swcollege.com).
3. Write an executive summary (200–250 words). As an administrative assistant to a busy executive, you are expected to summarize selected articles and present important points. You will find a model executive summary on the Web site.
4. Summarize this article (100–125 words) for your company's newsletter. You will find a model newsletter article on the Web site.
5. Review one or more of the Web sites mentioned in the story. What did you find useful? Your instructor may ask you to share your results in a five-minute presentation or one-page memo.
6. Write an electronic résumé. How did you adapt your résumé for electronic presentation? Your instructor may ask you to share your results in a five-minute presentation or one-page memo.

BUILDING RESEARCH SKILLS

1. Post your résumé on three Web sites. In addition to those mentioned in the story, university career centers and your instructor may suggest other sites. Which sites did you like and why? What types of responses did you receive to your postings?
2. Individually or in teams, draft an electronic job-hunting guide. Your instructor may ask you to submit a three- to five-page guide or post a Web page, along with a letter of transmittal explaining the project.
3. Using at least three other references (books, journal articles, newspaper stories, magazine stories or credible Web sites) write an 800- to 1,000-word essay addressing two of the preceding critical thinking questions. Assume that this essay will be used as an internal reference for a corporation's Internet manual.

4.   Using at least three other references (books, journal articles, newspaper stories, magazine stories or credible Web sites) post an 800- to 1,000-word Web page addressing at least two of the preceding critical thinking questions. Assume that this page will be posted on a corporate intranet.

College and Money:
And Never Lie About Your Grades
Nothing to do for the rest of your life? Don't panic.
When the recruiter calls, know your weakness,
think logically . . .

By Andrew Ross Sorkin

At first glance, the letter seemed promising. "We have reviewed your background and are impressed with your accomplishments," wrote Martha Day Smalley, the recruiting coordinator for the consulting firm McKinsey & Company. "However, we are unable to offer you the opportunity to interview with us." With one sentence, the door is slammed shut, any hope of an interview dashed.

As graduation looms, seniors across the country jockeying for jobs are waking up in a cold sweat at the prospect of receiving one of those dreaded thin, white envelopes. The recurring nightmare: "We have carefully considered your application in relation to our needs and have determined that we are unable to continue employment discussions with you," as Anderson Consulting puts it.

But students don't need to lose that much sleep. The job market for the class of 1999 is expected to be 10 percent greater than last year's, according to the National Association of Colleges and Employers, a nonprofit group in Bethlehem, Pa., that tracks hiring trends. For sophomores and juniors, summer-internship opportunities are also on the rise.

Computer science graduates, who are being offered an average starting salary of $44,878, are the most sought-after job applicants, according to the association. Engineering majors, particularly mechanical ($42,543), are in demand as well, followed by accounting ($33,477) and economics and finance ($35,016) majors. Though recruiting starts early for the most competitive fields, job counselors say it is not really too late for students just beginning the hunt, especially in liberal arts (starting salary: $25,000 to $30,000).

So how do you get your foot in the door and avoid the rejection letter? How do you negotiate the on-campus recruiting frenzy? Experts suggest the following strategies to students hunting for internships or that first real job.

STEP 1: KNOW THY FIELD

"Research, research, research!" exclaimed Robert W. Thirsk, the director of career services at Stanford University. "I can't tell you how many people walk in the door, and you say, 'What do you really think an analyst does?' and they have no idea," said Eleni D. Henkel, the principal and head of the Global Investment Banking Analyst program at Morgan Stanley Dean Witter. Talk to friends or family members who work in the field. Go on the Internet; almost every company has a Web site.

If you don't know anyone in your field, career-services departments can supply a list of alumni who work in a particular industry. Today, the buzzword in college job hunting is "information interview." Contact an alumnus and ask if you can meet for half an hour.

"Explain that you're looking for information and advice and that you are not applying for a job," said Patricia Rose, the director of career services at the University of Pennsylvania. Alumni are often approachable, and a meeting may be more than informative—it may lead to a job later.

If you have no connections but can muster the guts to make a cold call, find out who is in charge of a company's recruiting and ask for a half-hour meeting or even a brief phone conversation. More often than not, recruiters admire such persistence and agree to talk about their company.

STEP 2: KEEP IT SHORT

Students tend to compensate for their limited experience by inflating the length of their résumés. Across the board, recruiters agree that résumés should be only one page (that doesn't mean reducing the font size to anything smaller than 10 points, though). And unless applying for a very creative position, avoid fancy fonts and loud paper.

Recruiters also recommend omitting the traditional "objective" at the top. It wastes precious space, and you may accidentally send a company a résumé with the wrong objective—that is, one meant for another kind of job. (Recruiters say it happens all the time.) The consensus is that the cover letter is the most effective place to state your objective.

"I actually don't think an objective is helpful at all," said Ms. Henkel, adding that she spends an average of five minutes reading each cover letter and résumé that comes across her desk. "I prefer just to get more meat about the person."

Work or volunteer experiences should be in a sequence that makes sense to the field being pursued. If you volunteered in Tanzania for a summer and want a job in social services, that work may be more relevant than a summer job as a waitress. But if you're pursuing a career in hospitality, the waitressing job might be more important.

In most situations, it is important to include your grade point average. Obviously, a great one can be flaunted. But you can try to disguise one that isn't so hot. For example, if the G.P.A. in your major is higher than your overall G.P.A., label it and list it next to the overall one. If your junior- and senior-year grades are higher than your overall average, calculate the G.P.A. for those years and list it. The point is to show improvement, or success in a particular area. Be sure to also take the G.P.A. to two decimal places—don't round it—as those two points are significant when comparing averages. And never lie about your grades, as you will almost certainly get caught.

For jobs in finance or computer science, including your G.P.A. is imperative. "When I look at a résumé, and I'm reviewing it, and I see no G.P.A., I'm assuming the worst," Ms. Henkel said. "You didn't put it down, which means it must be really bad." For careers in publishing or marketing, it may not be necessary to include a G.P.A., especially for graduates of top-flight schools. If there is any question—and your G.P.A. is low—leave it off if applying for a position that doesn't include number crunching.

Finally, résumé writers often overlook hobbies and activities. "If you enjoy hiking, or you've traveled around the world, or you're a pilot, or whatever it is, put it in," Ms. Henkel said. "It's just something else that creates interesting conversation and catches your eye when you're reviewing résumés."

STEP 3: SHOW UP

"There are so many firms that have chosen to come and use on-campus recruiting early in the year, and so it leaves students thinking, 'Oh, my God, it's all done by the time they stop coming,'" said Beverly Hamilton-Chandler, the director of career services at Princeton University. "But that is never the case. We see students still getting jobs over the summer, but it means making overtures to companies now."

Typically, universities invite companies to their campus in the fall, and sometimes again in the spring, for job fairs or to stage dog-and-pony shows called information sessions. Investment banks, consulting firms and technology companies put on glitzy, often overwhelming, job fairs in the fall at a few larger schools. The big companies tend to have an enormous turnover. They start courting seniors early, partly because they have a general idea how many new employees they will need that hiring season. Other industries, like advertising, publishing, social services, law services and government, tend to recruit in the spring, and some don't recruit on campus actively because of the small number of positions available.

By mid-April, if you want a job in banking or consulting, quickly make a phone call to your top choices and send a cover letter and résumé by overnight mail to demonstrate your serious intentions.

For a schedule of fairs, contact your school's career-services department. An on-line virtual career fair, for instance, is being held later this month for Ivy League students. (The Web address and timing are not being disclosed to keep the fair limited to Ivy Leaguers.)

Bring several copies of your résumé to the on-campus fairs, and dress in the type of attire you would expect to wear on the job. Get to the fair early, before the lines start, so you can spend some quality time with a potential employer without having 10 people breathing down your neck. By mid-afternoon, most job fairs are packed.

First introduce yourself, then ask an open-ended, prepared question that gives the recruiter a chance to create a dialogue with you. "Let them know, 'I've done my homework,' without being too obnoxious," said Greg Knowles, the vice president and manager of university and student relations of the Chase Manhattan Corporation, who advised against asking anything too specific about something in the news or, worse, the company's annual report. Such questions smack of pretension, and can embarrass the recruiter if he or she is not as up-to-date as you.

And if you're really interested in an employer, return to the company's booth to say goodbye before leaving the fair—it leaves an impression.

A job fair is where shrinking violets must practice talking to people. Spend time watching others ask questions to see what works best. According to the National Association of Colleges and Employers, employers rate communication skills as the most important quality in hiring decisions involving undergraduates, followed by work experience (likely provided by a summer internship).

While most smaller schools don't have job fairs, companies often hold on-campus information sessions. "It's an opportunity to network, and an opportunity to find out more about the people who work for the company," Mr. Knowles said. "Would I enjoy working with these people every day?"

When sessions are over, most recruiters talk with one another about candidates they met at the presentation. It is crucial that you sign the guest book: companies often cross-reference these with résumés to gauge applicants' interest in them. At some competitive firms, you will be removed from the running if your name is not in the guest book.

If you can't make it to a presentation but are really interested in the company, send a note of apology. A word of caution: it has become increasingly common for students to sign in friends who never attended the presentation. Clearly, this verboten practice is not only unethical, but foolish. Unless the presentation has had hundreds of attendees, recruiters know who was there and who was not.

If you talked to a recruiter at a career fair or information session, send a thank-you note. A handwritten one is preferable, but even a typed letter will do.

BINGO! THE INTERVIEW

Once you have dropped off or sent your résumé to a company, the ball is in their court. They might invite you for an interview, or they might summarily reject you with one of those horrific thin envelopes. But even if you receive a rejection, your relationship is not necessarily over.

"There are some folks who are very persistent and really lobby," Ms. Henkel said. "There have been cases where someone will squeeze someone in for 15 minutes at the end of the day."

If you win the opportunity to interview, be prepared for anything from a pleasant chat to the grueling to the utterly bizarre.

Have answers ready for the lob-ball questions: "Where do you want to be in 5, 10 years?" "Why are your grades low?" "What are your weaknesses?"

The "What's your weakness?" question often turns into a self-made trap. Never say anything too indictable, and never, never, say you don't have a weakness.

Interview styles are industry-specific. For social-service jobs, recruiters might ask you about yourself and some of the experiences listed on your résumé. Publishing or public relations interviews are similar, though some companies want writing samples or may ask you to write something on the fly. Recruiters for jobs in advertising or marketing might throw out a couple of how-creative-are-you situations by giving you a product and asking you how to market it.

The hardest questions come from the most competitive fields—investment banking, management consulting and technology firms. These recruiters love to ask impossible-to-answer "case" questions like, "How many golf balls are sold in the United States each year?" What they never tell you is that you aren't expected to come up with the right answer. They are more interested in how you approach the problem, what logic you apply and how you respond under pressure.

To answer the golf ball question, estimate the percentage of golfers in the country, then come up with a concrete number using a known quantity like the population. From there, guess at how often, on average, a golfer golfs every month or week. Then determine the average number of balls a golfer uses each outing. You might also estimate how many balls are bought by ranges and miniature-golf companies.

Again, the point is not to calculate a number that is even remotely realistic. The interviewer just wants to hear you go through the different steps of accounting.

The best way to answer such questions is to practice. Talk to friends about what they have been asked. There are also a slew of Web sites and how-to books with practice questions.

The other type of posed problem—called a brain teaser—is significantly harder to prepare for because there is no formula. For example, interviewers have been known to ask, "Why are manhole covers round?" There are two ways to attack such questions: fire back with a witty answer and hope the interviewer laughs, or approach it as thoughtfully as possible. No matter what, don't give up.

(By the way, manhole covers are round because a circle is the only shape that can't be dropped into a same-shaped hole.)

"MEASURE WATER, GET A JOB"

This question has been used in student job interviews for ages; it has recently been posed by recruiters for Morgan Stanley Dean Witter.

Question: With one three-gallon jug and one five-gallon jug, how would you measure exactly four gallons of water?

Answer: (1) Fill the three-gallon jug. (2) Pour the water into the five-gallon jug. (3) Fill the three-gallon jug again. (4) Pour the water into the bigger jug to fill the remaining two gallons, leaving one gallon in the smaller jug. (5) Empty the five-gallon jug. (6) Pour the remaining gallon into the five-gallon jug. (7) Fill the smaller jug again. (8) Pour the water into the bigger jug. (9) That jug now contains four gallons.

"WEIGH BALLS, GET A JOB"

Goldman Sachs, among other companies, likes to pose this situation Question. You are given seven Ping-Pong balls, six are equal in weight, one is heavier. How would you find the heavy ball, using a seesaw-style scale only twice?

Answer: (1) Place three balls on each side. If the scale remains even, the ball not on it is the heavy one. (2) If one side dips, the heavy ball is on that side. (3) Place one of those three balls on each side. If both sides are even, the ball not on the scale is heavier. (4) If one side dips, it contains the heavy ball.

The New York Times, April 1, 1999
http://www.nytimes.com/library/national/040499edlife-sorkin.html

CRITICAL THINKING QUESTIONS

1. What is the importance of researching a company? How should you research a company?
2. What information should, and should not be, included on your résumé? What other information should accompany your résumé?
3. What steps should you take before, during and after a job fair?
4. What steps should you take before, during and after an interview?

SHORT APPLICATION ASSIGNMENTS

1. In teams of three to five, or as a class, discuss your responses to the preceding critical thinking questions.

2. Prepare a one-page memo report (200–250 words) to your instructor in which you respond to the critical thinking questions and offer a final summary of the article. You will find a model one-page report on the Web site (nytimes.swcollege.com).

3. Write an executive summary (200–250 words). As an administrative assistant to a busy executive, you are expected to summarize selected articles and present important points. You will find a model executive summary on the Web site.

4. Summarize this article (100–125 words) for your company's newsletter. You will find a model newsletter article on the Web site.

5. Write a résumé and accompanying cover letter. Your instructor may assign you a company. How did you adapt your cover letter and résumé for the specific company? Your instructor may ask you to share your results in a five-minute presentation or one-page memo.

6. In teams of three to five or individually, write a few interviewing questions, ranging from pleasant to grueling to the utterly bizarre. Next, role play with other teams or individuals. Try to be interviewer and interviewee at least once.

BUILDING RESEARCH SKILLS

1. Individually or in teams, draft a job-hunting guide. Your instructor may ask you to submit a three- to five-page guide or post a Web page, along with a letter of transmittal explaining the project.

2. Using at least three other references (books, journal articles, newspaper stories, magazine stories or credible Web sites) write an 800- to 1,000-word essay addressing two of the preceding critical thinking questions. Assume that this essay is a background document for a corporation's marketing plan.

3. Using at least three other references (books, journal articles, newspaper stories, magazine stories or credible Web sites) post an 800- to 1,000-word Web page addressing at least two of the preceding critical thinking questions. Assume that this page is a background document for a corporation's marketing plan.